STOIC
ALCHEMIST

**Transforming Lives
Through
Ancient Wisdom**

Jason Robinson

DNA Influence Publishing
www.dnainfluence.com

Library Data

Name: Robinson, Jason
Title Stoic Alchemist Transforming Lives Through Ancient Wisdom / Jason Robinson
Description: DNA Influence Publishing, 2023
Subject: Stoicism-Philosophy | Alchemy-Philosophy | Life Support & Guidance
Classification: Print | ebook

Printed & bound in the UK by Ingram sparks

Text Design by DNA Influence Publishing
This book was typeset in Garamond with Agency FB used as display fonts

To send correspondence to the author of this book, send an email to shift@stoicalchemist.com

www.stoicalchemist.com

Stoic Alchemy

Transforming Lives Through Ancient Wisdom!

'Embrace the alchemical process. Unleash your inner power.
Transform your life.' – Jason Robinson

CONTENTS

PART 5

CONCLUSION

Introduction

As a man, a dad, and a human, I understand life can be
overwhelming at times. Balancing work and family, managing
finances and responsibilities, and finding time for personal growth
and development can all be challenging. Stoic alchemy is a concept
that can help men in these situations find balance, connection, and
purpose in their lives. I created the term to express the shift people
take during their own personal journeys. The shift usually consists
of physical, psychological, emotional, and situational discomfort
during their time and life, but in the spirit of Stoic Alchemy, we
learn to transmute our thoughts to understand that moments of
discomfort are the true moments of growth and necessity.

We use Stoicism from its roots as an ancient philosophy that
teaches the importance of rational thought, self-control, and virtue.
Alchemy, on the other hand, is the transformation of the self
through spiritual and material practices. By combining these two
concepts, we can create a framework for personal growth and
development that can help men become better fathers, husbands,
and entrepreneurs.

In this book, we will explore the concepts of Stoic alchemy in
depth, including what Stoicism and alchemy are, the importance of
connection and balance, and the paradoxical nature of life. At the
end of each chapter, we will provide WARRIOR
ASSIGNMENTS. These are actionable tasks that you can
implement in your life to improve your well-being and growth, and
develop your inner Stoic Warrior!

WARRIOR ASSIGNMENT: Keep a daily Stoic journal where you
reflect on Stoic teachings and how they apply to your life as a dad,
a partner, a business owner, a worker and a human. Write down
your thoughts, insights, and struggles, and use this journal as a tool
for self-reflection and growth throughout the following chapters.

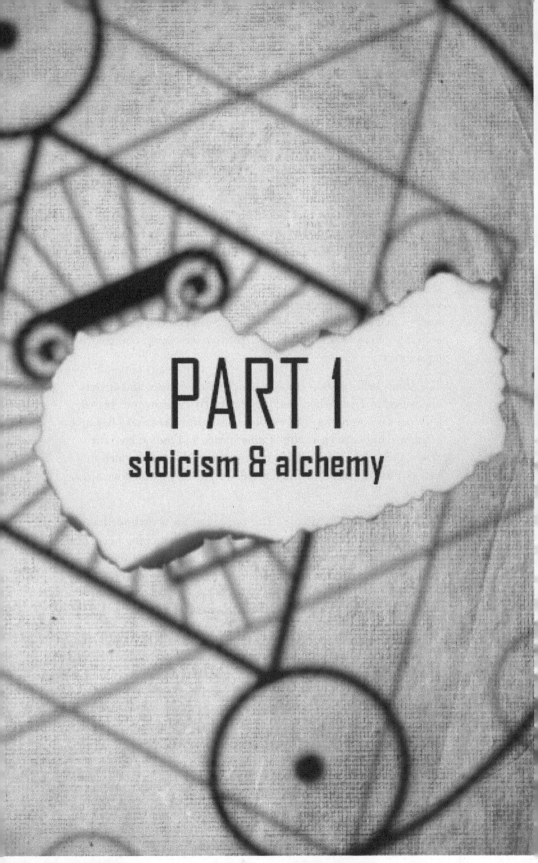

PART 1
stoicism & alchemy

ENTRY 1

What is Stoicism?

Stoicism is a school of philosophy that originated in ancient Greece and was founded by Zeno of Citium in the early 3rd century BC. The philosophy teaches that virtue, which is achieved through rationality and wisdom, is the highest good and that everything else is indifferent. This includes material possessions, external circumstances, and even our physical bodies. Stoicism teaches that we should focus on what we can control, namely our own thoughts and actions, and accept what we cannot control with equanimity.

The Stoics believed that emotions such as anger, fear, and anxiety are caused by false beliefs and judgments. By changing our beliefs and focusing on reason and virtue, we can overcome these negative emotions and achieve a state of inner peace and tranquility. The Stoics also believed in living in accordance with nature, which they saw as a harmonious and interconnected system of which we are a part of.

WARRIOR ASSIGNMENT: This one is not for everybody but works for many people which makes it worth mentioning here. Practice negative visualisation, which involves imagining the worst-case scenario in a given situation and then mentally preparing yourself for it. This can help you develop greater resilience and emotional fortitude in the face of challenges and setbacks.

Stoics belief that everything that happens in life is predetermined by fate, and that the only thing we can control is our own reactions to events is an interesting concept that requires deeper discussion around the meanings of fate and that if, as they believed that by cultivating virtues such as wisdom, courage, justice, and self-control, we can lead a life of happiness and fulfilment, does this shift us to controlling our fate or is our perception on life more important than the fate we are so destined to believe? This is a question we delve deeper into during our conversations during the paradox section.

One of the most famous Stoic philosophers was Marcus Aurelius, who was also a Roman emperor. He wrote in his book "Meditations" that "the happiness of your life depends upon the quality of your thoughts." This quote encapsulates the essence of Stoicism - that our thoughts and reactions to events are the key to our happiness. Thus, the re-wording and use of this thought train creates the famous quote "cheerfulness in the face of adversity!" Commonly used by the British Royal Marines Commandos.

As your read this book there are three ideologies of stoicism that I would like you to embody, something that all Stoic Warriors should meditate on with all life situations, these are:

1. The Dichotomy of Control: This philosophy, which emphasizes focusing on what is within our control and accepting what is outside of our control, originated with the stoic philosopher Epictetus.

2. The View from Above: This philosophy encourages individuals to take a step back and view their lives and situations from a broader perspective, as if they were looking down on them from a high point. This approach was championed by the stoic philosopher Marcus Aurelius.

3. Amor Fati: This philosophy, which translates to "love of fate," encourages individuals to accept and embrace all events in their lives, including the challenging and difficult ones. This stoic principle was promoted by the philosopher Friedrich Nietzsche, who was influenced by stoic philosophy.

For the purposes of my angle through this book, being in a stoic state is a moment of contemplation and philosophy. Being able to question conventional though and even your own beliefs ahead of the belief itself, taking you above your perception and allowing a projection of impartiality.

The people of stoicism have at times been described as 'someone who can endure pain or hardship without showing their feelings or complaining', also commonly termed as 'stoic faced' which is someone who shows no emotion. This is not the belief I hold.

I see Stoicism as a process of surrender, contemplation, understanding, control, and acceptance of the emotions, thoughts, and body rather than a lack of expression, and by the end of this I hope you can feel the same.

Here are a few of my favourite stoic philosophies to take into your day with you:

1. "You have power over your mind - not outside events. Realize this, and you will find strength." - Marcus Aurelius

2. "We suffer more often in imagination than in reality." - Seneca

3. "We should always be asking ourselves: Is this something that is, or is not, in my control?" - Epictetus

4. "No person has the power to have everything they want, but it is in their power not to want what they don't have, and to cheerfully put to good use what they do have." - Seneca

5. "Freedom is not the right to live as we please, but the right to find how we ought to live in order to fulfil our potential." - Epictetus

6. "The greater the difficulty, the more glory in surmounting it. Skilful pilots gain their reputation from storms and tempests." - Epictetus

7. "Waste no more time arguing what a good man should be. Be one." - Marcus Aurelius

8. "The greatest wealth is to live content with little." - Plato

These particular Stoic philosophies can be applied in various areas of life, including personal development, decision-making, and overcoming challenges.

WARRIOR ASSIGNMENT: Study the works of Stoic philosophers such as Marcus Aurelius, Seneca, and Epictetus, and try to apply their teachings to your daily life. Consider joining a Stoic reading group or online community to deepen your understanding and connect with like-minded individuals.

Throughout the book I will be creating actionable tasks for you to muse, practice and incorporate into your lifestyle. This is to allow you to manage certain elements of the book and create questions to answer and answers to questions throughout our time together and continued into your life as a ritual practice, allowing your intuition to switch on and solve problems, giving you access to rely more prominently on that 'gut feeling'. These will from now on be known as 'WARRIOR ASSIGNMENTS'! These tasks will be simple and instantly actionable!

WARRIOR ASSIGNMENT - this one will begin that deeper conversation with both sides of the brain: Start a gratitude journal. Each day, write down three things that you are grateful for. This practice can help you focus on the positive aspects of your life and cultivate a mindset of gratitude.

ENTRY 2

A brief introduction to Alchemy

"Alchemy is the art of transformation, the alchemist the vessel of change, and the pursuit of wisdom the philosopher's stone." - Unknown

Alchemy, on the other hand, is an ancient practice that has its roots in Egypt, China, and India. The alchemists were interested in the transformation of matter and the search for the philosopher's stone. However, alchemy developed into a pursuit of a spiritual dimension which is where the practice took its truest form, as the transformation of matter was seen as a metaphor for the transformation of the self.

As an ancient philosophical and proto-scientific tradition, it has a rich and diverse history that spans thousands of years. Rooted in the quest for knowledge and the pursuit of transformation, alchemy has captivated the minds of individuals throughout different civilizations and epochs. In this exploration of alchemy's history, we will delve into key moments, notable figures, and significant contributions that shaped the evolution of this enigmatic discipline.

The origins of alchemy can be traced back to ancient Egypt, where it emerged around 3000 BCE. The Egyptian alchemists, known as "chemists" or "khem," sought to understand the nature of matter and its transformation. They believed in the concept of the "Great Work" or the "Philosopher's Stone," a substance with the power to transmute base metals into gold and grant immortality.

Alchemy reached its pinnacle in the Hellenistic period, particularly in the cities of Alexandria and Antioch. During the 3rd and 4th centuries BCE, alchemists like Zosimos of Panopolis and Maria the Jewess made significant contributions to alchemical knowledge. Zosimos explored the spiritual and symbolic aspects of alchemy, while Maria is credited with inventing several alchemical apparatus and refining distillation techniques.

In the Islamic Golden Age, which spanned from the 8th to the 14th centuries, alchemy flourished and experienced profound advancements. Islamic alchemists, such as Jabir ibn Hayyan (known as Geber in the West) and Al-Razi (Rhazes), made ground-breaking discoveries in chemistry, medicine, and metallurgy. Jabir, considered the father of Islamic alchemy, developed a sophisticated system of laboratory techniques and apparatus and contributed to the understanding of chemical processes.

Alchemy continued to evolve during the European Middle Ages, where it became intertwined with religious and mystical beliefs. Prominent figures like Albertus Magnus, Roger Bacon, and Ramon Llull incorporated alchemy into their philosophical and scientific pursuits. Their works laid the foundation for the subsequent development of Western alchemy.

The Renaissance period marked a resurgence of alchemical interest, with figures such as Paracelsus and Heinrich Khunrath playing significant roles. Paracelsus, a Swiss physician and alchemist, rejected the traditional views of alchemy and emphasised the importance of observation and experimentation in the pursuit of knowledge. Khunrath, a German physician and alchemist, authored influential alchemical texts and integrated spiritual and religious elements into his work.

Going back to the beginning, one of the most influential alchemists in history is Hermes Trismegistus, often regarded as the legendary founder of alchemy. His writings, known as the Hermetic Corpus, had a profound impact on alchemical and philosophical thought. The Corpus Hermeticum presented a holistic worldview that blended spiritual, cosmological, and alchemical principles.

The 17th and 18th centuries witnessed a shift in alchemy's trajectory with the emergence of modern science and the rise of rationalism. Alchemical pursuits began to merge with early chemistry, leading to the development of more systematic and empirical approaches to understanding matter and chemical transformations. Figures like Robert Boyle and Isaac Newton, known for their contributions to modern science, were also influenced by alchemical ideas.

In the 19th and 20th centuries, alchemy experienced a revival in various forms. Theosophical societies, influenced by Eastern philosophies, embraced alchemical concepts as part of their spiritual teachings. Figures like Carl Jung explored alchemy's psychological symbolism and its relevance to the process of individuation and personal transformation.

Today, while the traditional practice of alchemy has largely faded, its legacy endures in the form of metaphorical and symbolic interpretations. Alchemy continues to inspire and captivate individuals seeking deeper understanding and personal growth. Its principles of transformation, transmutation, and inner alchemy resonate with those on the path of self-discovery.

In the words of Hermes Trismegistus, "As above, so below; as within, so without." This timeless maxim encapsulates the essence of alchemy, reminding us that the keys to understanding the universe and ourselves lie in the harmonious interplay of the inner and outer realms.

So, in the term Stoic Alchemy we are implementing the idea of the transformation of the self through spiritual and material practices. The practices and philosophies we will work with and begin to understand have been around for centuries and have transmuted within themselves to allow for different cultures and beliefs to incorporate them deeply into their wholistic and spiritual ways of life.

In the Western tradition, alchemy became associated with the work of medieval European alchemists such as Paracelsus, who believed that the human body was a microcosm of the universe, and that health was achieved through a balance of the four elements (earth, air, fire, and water) and the three principles (sulfur, mercury, and salt). Alchemy also had a mystical dimension, as the search for the philosopher's stone eventually became a quest for spiritual enlightenment and union with the divine.

The alchemist's goal is to achieve a state of spiritual enlightenment by working on oneself through various practices such as meditation, yoga, or other forms of spiritual practice. The alchemist also seeks to balance the material and spiritual aspects of life, recognising that both are important for personal growth and development. It is a process that will never be complete, and in its own practice teaches us that the journey is more important than the goal!

WARRIOR ASSIGNEMNT: Start a daily meditation practice. Spend at least 10 minutes each day in quiet contemplation. This practice can help you become more mindful, and present and can also help reduce stress and anxiety in turn transmuting the energies of stress to the energies of control. There are no specific instructions with this, as it is about creating the space and time first, once you have calved out this it can become more than a 10-minute meditation.

In a modern context, Stoicism and alchemy can be seen as complementary approaches to personal growth and development. Both philosophies emphasize the importance of inner transformation and the cultivation of virtues such as wisdom, courage, and compassion. They also encourage us to focus on what is within our control and to let go of attachment to external circumstances and material possessions.

In a world that is increasingly fast-paced and connected, Stoicism and alchemy offer a counterbalance to the noise and distractions of modern life. By cultivating a sense of inner peace and tranquillity, we can navigate the challenges and obstacles that we inevitably face with greater resilience and equanimity. By focusing on inner transformation and personal growth, we can create a sense of purpose and meaning in our lives and find greater fulfilment and satisfaction.

In the following chapters, we will explore in more detail how the principles of Stoicism and alchemy can be applied in different areas of life, including our relationships, our work, and our personal well-being. We will also provide practical tips and exercises for incorporating these principles into our daily lives, and share stories and examples of men who have successfully applied these principles in their own lives.

WARRIOR ASSIGNMENT: Explore the concept of alchemy in your own life by identifying areas where you can transform negative emotions or experiences into something positive. For example, if you are feeling stressed or overwhelmed at work, try reframing the situation as an opportunity for growth and learning.

PART 2
connection

ENTRY 3

Connection

"Every human being has a basic instinct to help each other out. It might not seem that way sometimes, but it's true." - W.P. Kinsella

In today's world, many men struggle with finding a sense of purpose and belonging in life. The demands of work and family life can leave us feeling disconnected and adrift, with little time or energy to focus on our own needs and aspirations. However, by connecting with our intuition, finding our tribe, and connecting with nature, we can cultivate a sense of meaning and purpose that can sustain us through even the most challenging times.

Connection is an important part of Stoic alchemy. The Stoics believed that everything in the universe is connected, and that we are all part of a greater whole. This belief is similar to the concept of "oneness" in Eastern spirituality.

Connection can take many forms, such as connection to nature, connection to others, or connection to a higher power. By cultivating these connections, we can feel more grounded and centered, and can also develop a greater sense of purpose and meaning in life.

There are many aspects of connection and for this book, I will be going into the areas of Intuition I feel are the most important for a Stoic Warrior, intuition, tribe, and nature.

ENTRY 4

INTUITION

"The intuitive mind is a sacred gift and the rational mind is a faithful servant. We have created a society that honours the servant and has forgotten the gift." - Albert Einstein

Intuition is an important aspect of connection. The Stoics believed that intuition was a form of divine guidance, and that by listening to our inner voice, we can make better decisions in life.

Intuition is often described as a gut feeling or a sense of knowing that arises without conscious thought or analysis. While intuition can be difficult to define or quantify, many people believe that it is an important source of guidance and wisdom in our lives. In shamanic traditions, intuition is viewed as a powerful tool for accessing spiritual guidance and connecting with the natural world. Shamans believe that intuition arises from a deep connection to the spiritual realm and can be used to gain insight into the hidden aspects of reality.

In the Stoic Alchemy context, intuition is seen as an important element of the human experience, which can guide us towards fulfilling our purpose and living a more fulfilling life. Intuition can help us tap into our inner wisdom and connect with our true selves, allowing us to make decisions that are in alignment with our values and journey.

One of the key principles of Stoic Alchemy is to find balance between the material and spiritual aspects of our lives. This requires us to cultivate an awareness of our intuition, which can help us navigate the complexities of the material world while staying connected to our spiritual selves. In this way, intuition becomes a powerful tool for achieving balance and harmony in our lives.

Shamans often use various techniques to cultivate and access their intuition, such as meditation, dreamwork, and shamanic journeying.

Shamanic dreamwork and journeying are powerful tools used by shamans to access higher states of consciousness, connect with spiritual allies, and gain insight and wisdom. In shamanic dreamwork, the shaman enters a dream-like state while remaining awake and alert, allowing them to access the subconscious mind and explore the realms of the spirit world. This state of consciousness is often induced through rhythmic drumming or chanting, which helps to quiet the mind and shift the shaman's awareness.

During shamanic journeying, the shaman enters an altered state of consciousness, similar to a meditative state, in order to explore the spiritual realm and connect with spirit allies. This can be done through guided meditation, drumming, or other methods that help to induce an altered state of consciousness. Once in this state, the shaman is able to communicate with spirits, gain insights and wisdom, and receive guidance on their path.

Shamanic dreamwork and journeying are powerful tools for self-discovery, healing, and personal growth. By accessing higher states of consciousness and connecting with spiritual allies, the shaman is able to gain insight and wisdom that can help them overcome challenges and obstacles on their path and the path of their community. These practices also help to develop a deeper connection with the natural world, the spirit realm, and the self.

These practices are designed to help them connect with the spiritual realm and gain insight into the deeper aspects of reality. Similarly, Stoic Alchemy also encourages practices like meditation and self-reflection, which can help us tap into our intuition and connect with our inner wisdom.

Shamanism is and has been practiced for 10s of 1000s of years in different cultures all around the world. Although each culture has its own unique approach to shamanism, there are many common themes and practices that unite them.

In North America, indigenous tribes such as the Navajo, Apache, and Hopi have their own shamanic traditions. The Navajo call their shamans "medicine men" or "medicine women," while the Apache refer to them as "shamanisers." The Hopi have a similar tradition of shamanic healing, and their shamans are known as "kachinas."

In South America, shamanism is practiced by many indigenous cultures, including the Amazonian tribes. The Shipibo people of Peru have a rich shamanic tradition, and their shamans are known as "curanderos." The Quechua people of the Andes also have a tradition of shamanic healing, and their shamans are called "paqos."

In Siberia, shamanism has been practiced by the Tungus and other indigenous groups for thousands of years. Their shamans are known as "chukchi" or "tungus," and they are believed to have the ability to communicate with the spirits of animals and nature.

In Africa, shamanism is practiced by many different tribes, including the San people of southern Africa and the Dinka people of Sudan. The San people have a rich tradition of shamanic healing, and their shamans are known as "sangomas." The Dinka people also have a tradition of shamanic healing, and their shamans are called "witch doctors."

In Asia, shamanism has been practiced by many different cultures, including the Mongols, Koreans, and indigenous groups in Siberia. The Mongols have a tradition of shamanic healing, and their shamans are known as "bo" or "udgan." The Koreans also have a tradition of shamanism, and their shamans are called "mudang."

Despite the many different names and approaches to shamanism, there are many common themes that unite them. As mentioned most shamanic traditions involve the use of altered states of consciousness to connect with the spiritual realm, as well as the belief that everything in nature is alive and has its own spirit.

Shamans are also often called upon to perform healing and divination, and to help guide their community through difficult times.

Both shamanism and Stoic Alchemy recognize the importance of intuition as a tool for gaining insight into the deeper aspects of reality and connecting with the spiritual realm. By cultivating our intuition, we can tap into our inner wisdom and live a more balanced and fulfilling life, in alignment with our true selves and our purpose in the world.

Unfortunately, we are very different of the shaman of the past, and modern life often leaves little room for intuition. We are bombarded with information and stimuli from all directions, and it can be difficult to find moments of stillness and quiet in which our intuition can be heard. However, there are a number of practices and techniques that can help us cultivate our intuition and connect with our inner wisdom.

WARRIOR ASSIGNMENT: One such practice is mindfulness meditation, which involves paying attention to the present moment without judgment. We take the previous assignment of finding the space and time one step further by focusing our attention on our breath or other sensory experiences, we can quiet the chatter of our minds and create space for our intuition to emerge. Do not search for a quiet mind, let it come to you, it may not be quiet for a long time, just know that when you sit and thoughts come, just to observe them and let them be, don't answer them, just let them pass. Other practices such as journaling, spending time in nature, and engaging in creative activities can also help us tap into our intuition and connect with our inner selves.

With intuition comes the understanding of synchronicities. The concept of synchronicity, as introduced by Swiss psychiatrist Carl Jung, refers to meaningful coincidences that cannot be explained by causality. Many people who have studied or practiced Stoic philosophy and alchemy have noted the connection between these ideas and the experience of synchronicity.

Intuition, as we have discussed earlier, is a powerful tool for connecting with our inner selves and the world around us. It allows us to tap into a deeper level of awareness and gain insight that may not be available through rational thought alone. When we trust our intuition, we may be more open to recognizing and experiencing synchronicities.

From a scientific perspective, some research has suggested that synchronicity may be related to the concept of quantum entanglement, which describes how particles can be connected regardless of their physical distance from one another. This idea suggests that there may be a fundamental interconnectedness to the universe that allows for seemingly coincidental events to occur.

In the context of Stoic alchemy, the idea that nothing happens by accident can be seen as a way of accepting the world as it is and finding meaning in every experience. Rather than viewing events as random or chaotic, we can choose to see them as opportunities for growth and transformation. By practicing Stoic philosophy and connecting with our intuition, we may be more attuned to recognizing and embracing these opportunities.

Synchronicities can serve as a reminder that we are all connected, and that there may be a greater purpose or meaning to our lives than what we can see on the surface. By paying attention to these meaningful coincidences and trusting our intuition, we may be able to tap into a deeper level of wisdom and understanding.

WARRIOR ASSIGNMENT: Look for the synchronicities, if you are delayed or something negative happens, look for the balance and try to think why that could have happened. Maybe you were held up to avoid that crash that happened on the motorway!

ENTRY 5

TRIBE/COMMUNITY

"The longing for community is the desire to awaken the heart and restore its true nature." - Jack Kornfield

Another important aspect of connection is our tribe or community. Human beings are social creatures, and we thrive on connection with others. The people we surround ourselves with can greatly influence our thoughts, feelings, and behaviours. It's essential to choose our tribe wisely and cultivate relationships with people who share similar values and goals. In a world that can often feel fragmented and divided, having a sense of belonging to a community can be incredibly powerful and grounding.

Modern society has come a long way in terms of technological advancements and scientific discoveries. However, in our pursuit of progress, we have lost touch with the wisdom and knowledge of ancient tribes who lived in harmony with nature and each other. These tribes, who still exist today in some remote parts of the world, have developed a deep understanding of the interconnectedness of all things and the importance of balance in all aspects of life. By learning from their ways, modern society could benefit greatly.

Linking to our forthcoming part on nature, finding a tribe that is in harmony with all living things and if we look for ancient tribal wisdom is in our relationship with the environment it will allow for our own personal growth immensely. Many ancient tribes see themselves as stewards of the land, with a deep respect for the natural world and an understanding of the impact that human actions can have on the environment. By adopting a similar approach, modern society could reduce our impact on the environment and ensure a sustainable future for generations to come.

Additionally, ancient tribal cultures often have a strong sense of community and interconnectedness, which is something that modern society lacks. Many people today feel isolated and disconnected, despite the prevalence of social media and technology. By taking a page from ancient tribal cultures and fostering a sense of community and interconnectedness, modern society could improve mental health and overall well-being.

Furthermore, ancient tribes have developed various practices and rituals that help to cultivate a deeper sense of purpose and meaning in life. For example, shamanic practices such as dreamwork and journeying can help individuals connect with their inner wisdom and intuition and gain a greater understanding of their place in the world. By incorporating similar practices into our lives, we can improve our overall sense of fulfilment and purpose.

Modern society has much to learn from ancient tribal cultures. By adopting their wisdom and practices, we can improve our relationship with the environment, foster a greater sense of community and interconnectedness, and cultivate a deeper sense of purpose and meaning in life. It is time for us to look to the past in order to create a better future for all.

Here are some great benefits of having a community:

Sure, here are 10 benefits to being a part of a community:

1. Emotional support: Being part of a community provides emotional support. It allows individuals to share their experiences, feelings, and problems with like-minded individuals.

2. Sense of belonging: A community provides a sense of belonging and identity, which can be particularly beneficial for those who feel isolated or disconnected.

3. Social interaction: Being part of a community provides opportunities for social interaction and engagement, which can help reduce loneliness and social isolation.

4. Knowledge sharing: A community provides a platform for knowledge sharing and collaboration, which can lead to personal and professional growth.

5. Increased self-confidence: Being part of a community can help individuals build self-confidence and self-esteem. When individuals feel supported and valued, they are more likely to take risks and pursue their goals.

6. Networking opportunities: A community provides networking opportunities that can be beneficial for professional development.

7. Shared resources: Being part of a community provides access to shared resources such as information, tools, and expertise.

8. Opportunities for collaboration: Being part of a community provides opportunities for collaboration and partnerships.

9. Sense of purpose: Being part of a community can give individuals a sense of purpose and meaning. When individuals are working towards a common goal or purpose, they are more likely to feel fulfilled and satisfied.

10. Improved physical health: Being part of a community can lead to improved physical health through increased social interaction, community events, and group challenges.

Men, in particular, benefit from being part of a community of other men. This is not to say that men cannot have strong bonds with women, but there is something uniquely powerful about the connection between men.

Historically, men have formed tight-knit communities for a variety of reasons, including survival, protection, and mutual support. In Viking society, for example, men would band together to form small communities known as "hofs" or "heaths." These communities were essential for the Vikings' way of life, which was characterized by exploration, trade, and warfare. The men in these communities relied on each other for protection, sustenance, and companionship. They shared a common purpose and a shared sense of identity.

Today, men face many of the same challenges as their Viking ancestors, albeit in different forms. Many men struggle with issues related to masculinity, such as identity, purpose, and connection. They may feel isolated or disconnected from others, especially other men. They may feel pressure to conform to societal norms or expectations around what it means to be a "real man." They may also feel ashamed or vulnerable about their emotions, fearing that expressing them will make them appear weak or unmanly.

This is where communities of men can play a vital role. By coming together with other men, men can find a space where they can be themselves, free from judgment or expectations. They can share their experiences, their fears, and their hopes with others who understand what they are going through. They can form deep bonds of trust and support that can sustain them through difficult times.

Research has shown that being part of a community of men can have numerous benefits, including:

1. Improved mental health: Men who are part of a community report higher levels of emotional well-being and lower rates of depression and anxiety.

2. Increased resilience: Men who have a strong network of support are better able to handle stress and adversity.

3. Enhanced sense of purpose: Men who are part of a community report feeling more connected to a larger purpose or mission.

4. Improved physical health: Men who are part of a community tend to be more physically active and take better care of their health.

5. Increased creativity: Men who are part of a community often report feeling more inspired and motivated to pursue creative endeavours.

6. Improved communication skills: Men who spend time with other men are better able to express their thoughts and feelings and listen to others.

7. Greater sense of belonging: Men who are part of a community report feeling more connected to others and to the world around them.

8. Increased accountability: Men who are part of a community can hold each other accountable for their actions and behavior.

9. Enhanced problem-solving skills: Men who are part of a community often have access to a wide range of knowledge and expertise, making it easier to solve problems and find solutions.

10. Increased sense of brotherhood: Men who are part of a community often report feeling a strong sense of brotherhood and camaraderie, which can be deeply fulfilling and satisfying.

Being part of a community of men can have a profound impact on your life. By coming together with other men, you can find a sense of connection, purpose, and belonging that is essential to your well-being. The Viking communities provide an excellent example of how men have come together throughout history to form formidable communities, and we as modern men can learn from their example.

A tribe or community means caring for others and helping when others are in need. We are all humans and in turn are one big tribe. Unfortunately, we have be divided and pit against each other in some areas of life as is the human condition, and for this we just need to be ready to help those in our communities and anyone outside of them with an open mind.

It is often said that one of the greatest sources of happiness in life is helping others. Whether it's through volunteering, giving to charity, or simply doing something kind for someone else, there is something inherently rewarding about making a positive impact on another person's life.

But did you know that there is also a scientific basis for this phenomenon? Research has shown that helping others can actually trigger the release of certain hormones in the brain that can lead to increased creativity, happiness, and abundance in one's own life.

One of the hormones that is released when we help others is oxytocin. Oxytocin is often referred to as the "love hormone" because it is associated with feelings of bonding, trust, and empathy. When we help others, oxytocin is released in our brains, which can help us feel more connected to those around us and more motivated to continue helping others.

Another hormone that is released when we help others is dopamine. Dopamine is often referred to as the "reward hormone" because it is associated with feelings of pleasure and satisfaction. When we do something kind for someone else, dopamine is released in our brains, which can make us feel happier and more fulfilled.

But it's not just about the hormones. Helping others can also have a profound effect on our brains in other ways. For example, research has shown that doing things for others can actually help to connect the left and right hemispheres of the brain, which can lead to increased creativity and problem-solving abilities.

Additionally, helping others can help to reduce stress and improve overall well-being. When we focus on the needs of others, we are less likely to dwell on our own problems and concerns, which can help to reduce feelings of stress and anxiety.

In short, there are many benefits to helping others, both for the person being helped and the person doing the helping. By triggering the release of certain hormones in the brain and improving overall brain function, helping others can lead to increased happiness, creativity, and abundance in one's own life. So, the next time you have the opportunity to help someone else, remember that you're not just doing something good for them – you're also doing something good for yourself, and we all need to do a bit more for ourselves don't we Warriors!

Stoic Alchemy emphasizes the importance of cultivating deep, meaningful relationships with others. By developing a strong sense of connection with our tribe, we can feel more grounded, supported, and fulfilled in life. At the same time, our tribe can also serve as a source of accountability, challenging us to be our best selves and holding us accountable when we fall short.

WARRIOR ASSIGNMENT: Find a community that aligns with your values and morals. One way to find your tribe is to seek out groups or organizations that align with your interests and values. This could be a professional association, a volunteer group, a sports team, or a spiritual community, among others. By connecting with others who share our passions and goals, we can find a sense of camaraderie and support that can help us navigate the challenges of daily life.

ENTRY 6

NATURE

"In every walk with nature, one receives far more than he seeks." - John Muir

Nature is also a powerful connection for Stoic Warriors. I believed that nature is a manifestation of divine reason and that we should live in harmony with it. Spending time in nature, practicing mindfulness, and observing the beauty and cycles of nature can be a powerful tool for personal growth and transformation.

Connecting with nature can be a unique way to restore our sense of balance and wellbeing. In today's world, many of us spend the majority of our time indoors, surrounded by artificial light, noise, and stimuli. However, research has shown that spending time in natural settings can have a host of positive effects on our physical, mental, and emotional health.

Some ways to connect with nature include taking walks or hikes in natural settings, practicing outdoor yoga or meditation, or simply spending time sitting outside and observing the natural world. By reconnecting with the natural world around us, we can cultivate a deeper sense of connection and belonging in the world.

Source and spirit are also integral to the Stoic Alchemist's understanding of connection. The Stoics believed that there is a higher power that governs the universe and that by aligning ourselves with it, we can achieve greater harmony and purpose in life. Whether you believe in this or not there are many physical and mental benefits beyond the spirit to connecting with nature.

Nature plays a vital role in Japanese culture, where it is considered a sacred and powerful force that influences all aspects of life. The Japanese have a deep reverence for nature, and their traditional religions, such as Shinto and Buddhism, incorporate a strong connection with the natural world.

For the Japanese, spending time in nature is seen as a way to recharge and find balance in life. The practice of "forest bathing," or shinrin-yoku, has become a popular way to connect with nature and promote health and well-being. It involves immersing oneself in a forest or natural setting and using the senses to fully experience and appreciate the surroundings.

Incorporating a similar practice of connecting with nature can be beneficial for you. Spending time in natural settings can help you to ground and centre, and provide a sense of calm and clarity. It can also inspire creativity and provide a space for reflection and contemplation.

The Stoic philosophy of recognizing the interconnectedness of all things also aligns with the Japanese concept of "mono no aware," or the bittersweet appreciation of the transience of things. This idea acknowledges the impermanence of all things in nature, and emphasizes the importance of cherishing each moment and being fully present in the present. This being beautifully aligned with the Japanese concept of "Wabi Sabi", which for me is an indescribable feeling of open heartedness in the presence of the imperfect beauty of nature. This term is beautifully written on in the book 'Wabi Sabi' by Beth Kempton, and is part of the inspiration to write this book.

By incorporating the Japanese reverence for nature and the practice of "forest bathing," you as a Stoic Warrior can deepen your connection with the natural world and find greater peace and harmony in life. This can lead to a greater appreciation for the interconnectedness of all things and a deeper sense of purpose and belonging in the world.

As well as forest bathing there is a practice called grounding, also known as earthing, it is a practice that involves physically connecting with the earth by walking barefoot on the ground or standing on it. This practice is believed to offer a number of health benefits, and has been used by cultures around the world for centuries.

One of the primary benefits of grounding is the way it helps to discharge excess electrical energy that builds up in the body. It is used as an part of the forest bathing, or shinrin-yoku experience. This electrical energy can come from a variety of sources, such as exposure to electronic devices, and can lead to feelings of stress and anxiety. Grounding is believed to help reduce this build-up of electrical energy and promote feelings of calmness and relaxation by exchanging the positively built-up ions for negative ones creating balance in the body once more.

Additionally, grounding improves the body's immune response, reduces inflammation, and improves sleep. It also helps to reduce chronic pain and improve circulation.

Grounding through barefoot contact with the earth can help you to connect and sync with nature, cultivate a sense of calm and inner peace, and promote a greater sense of mindfulness. By taking time to disconnect from technology and other distractions, and connecting with the earth through grounding, you can tap into a deeper sense of connection with the world around you, and unlock new levels of insight and understanding. To deepen that natural connection to nature we can explore the realms of the circadian rhythm.

The natural world is constantly in motion, and as humans, we are an integral part of this ecosystem. Our physical and mental well-being is closely connected to the rhythms and cycles of nature, including the daily cycle of light and darkness, known as the circadian rhythm. The circadian rhythm is a natural internal process that regulates the sleep-wake cycle, among other bodily functions.

As mentioned, many times, we have become increasingly disconnected from nature and its rhythms. We spend most of our time indoors, surrounded by artificial light and technology, and we often ignore the natural cues that our bodies receive from the environment. This can have a hugely negative impact on our physical and mental health, leading to sleep disturbances, hormonal imbalances, and even chronic diseases.

One way to reconnect with nature and sync with our circadian rhythm is through grounding as it allows us to absorb the Earth's energy and balance our own electrical charge.

In addition to grounding, spending time in natural settings can also help us sync with nature's rhythms. Exposure to natural light and darkness can help regulate our circadian rhythm, leading to better sleep and more balanced hormonal levels.

While everyone's circadian rhythm is unique, there are some general guidelines that can help us sync with nature's rhythms. It is recommended to expose ourselves to natural light and darkness as much as possible, particularly in the morning and evening hours.

The connection between humans and nature is essential to our physical and mental well-being and it can be hard to get out to places of nature when we live in this modern society, but incorporating natural elements into our daily lives can also be helpful, such as bringing plants into our homes or offices, or incorporating natural materials such as wood or stone into our living spaces. Additionally, reducing exposure to artificial light sources, particularly in the evenings, can help to promote better sleep and alignment with our circadian rhythms.

Overall, by reconnecting with the natural world and syncing with our circadian rhythms, we can experience a wide range of benefits for our physical and mental health. These benefits include improved sleep quality, greater energy and vitality, reduced stress and anxiety, and improved cognitive function. So, to improve your overall well-being, and connection to all natural elements consider spending more time in nature and paying attention to the rhythms of the natural world around you.

Stoic Alchemy emphasizes the importance of living in harmony with nature. By recognizing our connection to the natural world and living in accordance with its rhythms and cycles, we can live a more balanced and fulfilling life. This can include spending more time in nature, practicing mindfulness, and embracing simplicity.

WARRIOR ASSIGNMENT: Take a nature walk. Spend at least 30 minutes in nature, whether it's a park, a beach, or a hiking trail. Practice mindfulness and observe the beauty of nature around you. Consider how you can cultivate deeper connections with nature in your daily life.

There are many things which we find connection to. I do not wish you to confuse connection with attachment as attachment is a concept that holds a negative implication and can be deeply looked into in the book 'The Five Levels Of Attachment' by Don Miguel Ruiz Jr. I would however, like to briefly outline our sense of connection to also encompasses our relationship with the source of all things. Whether we call it Energy, Prana, Chi, Ki, God, the Universe, or something else entirely, the source is the ultimate reality that underlies all existence. By connecting with the source, we can tap into a deeper sense of meaning and purpose and find greater peace and fulfillment in life.

Stoic Alchemy recognizes the importance of cultivating a sense of connection with the source. This can involve spiritual practices such as meditation, prayer, or contemplation. By developing a deeper sense of connection with source, we can tap into a wellspring of inner wisdom and guidance and navigate life's challenges with greater ease and grace.

Our sense of connection also encompasses the relationship between spirit and the material world. As human beings, we exist at the intersection of the spiritual and the material. Our bodies are made of matter, but our consciousness is something more profound.

Stoic Alchemy recognizes the importance of finding balance between the spiritual and the material. By recognizing the interconnectedness of all things, we can find a deeper sense of harmony and balance in life. This can involve practices such as mindfulness, gratitude, and self-reflection.

The Stoic philosopher Epictetus once said, "First, tell yourself what kind of person you want to be. Then, do what you have to do." By cultivating a deep sense of connection with ourselves, with others, and with the natural world, we can align our actions with our values and live a life that is true to ourselves.

WARRIOR ASSIGNMENT: Take some time to reflect on your relationship with intuition, tribe, nature, source, and spirit. Are there areas where you could deepen your sense of connection? What practices could you incorporate into your daily routine to cultivate a deeper sense of connection with these aspects of life?

After looking deeply into the areas of connection and how we can integrate this principle through the areas of intuition, tribe, and nature you can begin to feel a sense of belonging within our very own tribe of Stoic Warriors. The understanding and philosophies of this book are the continuation of a journey that many of us men, dads, husbands, and business owners have always been on and only now beginning to take a fine grasp of to better our lives and those around us. To take ownership of our world and rise to a new world order of self-respect, self-love, and self-care.

GRAND WARRIOR ASSIGNMENT: Take time this week to connect with your intuition by practicing mindfulness meditation or engaging in a creative activity that speaks to your inner self. Additionally, seek out opportunities to connect with like-minded individuals by joining a group or organization that aligns with your interests and values. Finally, make a point to spend time in nature each day, even if it's just a few minutes spent sitting outside and observing the natural world around you.

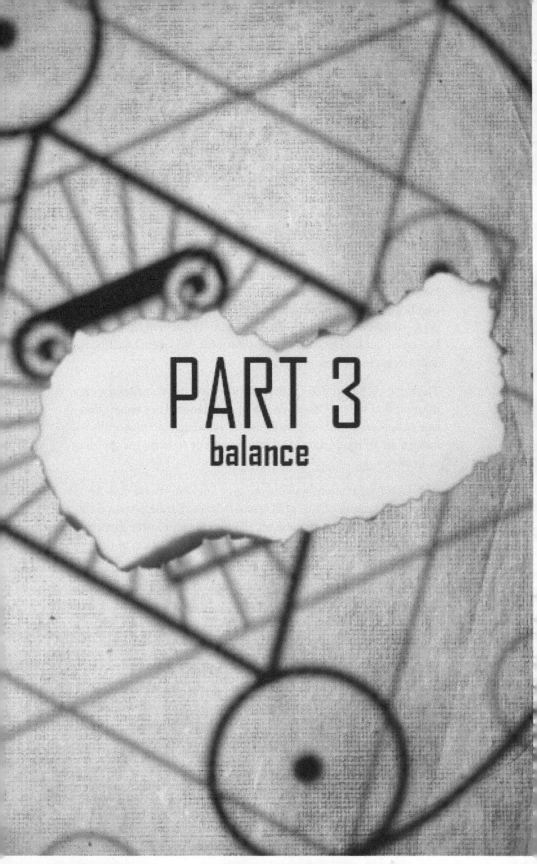

PART 3
balance

ENTRY 7

Balance

"The key is to keep company only with people who uplift you, whose presence calls forth your best." - Epictetus

As a man who has picked up this book, you are more than likely a dad or father to be and run a business of some sort. So, you will know or are soon to find out that finding balance in life can be a significant challenge. Balancing work and family responsibilities, personal interests, and self-care can feel overwhelming at times. However, cultivating balance is essential for our overall well-being and success in all areas of life.

The Stoics believed that finding balance involved cultivating a state of mind that was free from excess or deficiency. They taught that true happiness could only be found by avoiding extremes and living a life of moderation and self-control or to 'walk the grey line' as I call it.

Although I say it a lot, 'walking the grey line' can sound dull. So, the main takeaway of this is to create balance, but be prepared to fall off either side at any moment. To be a warrior in the gardener, instead of a gardener at war, and to be the nicest person in the room, but ready to die on the front line of your beliefs and morals.

In modern times, finding balance often involves navigating the tension between opposing forces. This can include finding a balance between our masculine and feminine energies, balancing our physical and mental health, and balancing our material and spiritual needs.

Balance is essential to living a healthy, fulfilling life. When we are out of balance, we may feel stressed, anxious, or overwhelmed. By finding a sense of balance, we can cultivate greater peace, harmony, and resilience in life.

Balance is our second key concept in Stoic Alchemy. Many ancient beliefs base their core principles around balance. The Stoics believed that balance was essential for personal growth and development, and that we should strive to find balance in all aspects of our lives, and some of the first known understandings of the universe that came from the Kybalion, 'The 7 Hermetic Principles' tend to swing many of the principles around the existence of extremes and finding harmony in the balance.

39

ENTRY 8

Masculine and Feminine Balance

"The wise man will love equally those who are in his care, and will bear with them all, but will not yield to them in matters of honour nor will he compromise his principles." - Epictetus

This quote suggests that the wise person will approach relationships with an open heart and mind, and treat everyone equally and with respect, regardless of gender or other factors. However, they will not compromise their own principles or values in order to please others or maintain a sense of social balance. This in itself requires a balanced approach of both masculine (assertiveness and honour) and feminine (compassion and love) qualities.

Thus, we discuss a hot topic of our current society that has been taken to its extreme and in this has lost balance. And the one thing we know about extremes is they are met with the alternate extreme and then both need to find balance.

Masculine and feminine energy is one aspect of balance that is often misunderstood. The Stoics recognized the importance of both masculine and feminine energy and believed that a balance between the two was essential for personal growth and development.

The concept of masculine and feminine energies has been around for thousands of years and is present in many spiritual and philosophical traditions. The Stoics believed that finding balance between these two energies was essential for cultivating a well-rounded and fulfilled life.

In modern times, the concept of balancing masculine and feminine energies is often associated with gender, but it is important to note that these energies are present in all individuals regardless of gender. Balancing masculine and feminine energies involves cultivating qualities such as strength, assertiveness, and leadership, while also nurturing qualities such as empathy, intuition, and creativity.

However, both aspects are essential and valuable, and a healthy balance of both is necessary for a fulfilling life and a well-rounded man. This balance can involve embracing both our own masculine and feminine aspects, as well as recognizing and valuing the masculine and feminine in others.

The masculine energy is associated with action, logic, and assertion, while the feminine energy is associated with intuition, creativity, and nurturing. For men, balancing these energies is essential to leading a fulfilling and purposeful life.

From a neurological perspective, the left brain is often associated with the masculine energy, while the right brain is associated with the feminine energy. The left brain is responsible for logic, reason, and analytical thinking (think straight lines), while the right brain is responsible for creativity, intuition, and emotional expression (think wavey and free). There are men that are more right brained, and women that are more left brained. This however, doesn't determine their sexual preference, career or life path, it is usually a result of conditioning and genetics. It does however, mean that you can work with the less dominant side to create more balanced thought process and connection.

This is also mirrored in the concept of yin and yang, rooted in traditional Chinese philosophy, emphasizes the importance of balancing opposing forces. Yin represents the feminine energy, characterized by darkness, coldness, and receptivity, while yang represents the masculine energy, characterized by light, warmth, and assertiveness. In order to achieve balance, one must acknowledge and embrace both yin and yang energies within themselves.

Similarly, the concept of light and dark also reflects the balance of masculine and feminine energies. Light represents the masculine energy, symbolizing clarity, reason, and order, while dark represents the feminine energy, symbolizing mystery, intuition, and chaos. Both light and dark energies are necessary for a complete understanding of oneself and the world around us.

When men learn to balance their masculine and feminine energies, they become more in touch with their intuition, creativity, and empathy. They are better able to communicate their emotions and connect with others on a deeper level. This balance allows for greater self-awareness and personal growth.

Furthermore, balancing masculine and feminine energies is not a one-size-fits-all approach. Each individual has their own unique balance of these energies, and it is up to the individual to discover and maintain that balance. This requires self-reflection, introspection, and a willingness to explore and embrace all aspects of oneself.

Balancing masculine and feminine energies is essential for men to live a fulfilling and purposeful life. By embracing both the left and right brain, yin and yang, and light and dark energies within themselves, men can become more in touch with their intuition, creativity, and empathy, leading to greater self-awareness and personal growth.

WARRIOR ASSIGNMENT: Explore your creative side by taking up a new hobby or passion project. This can help you tap into your inner muse and find greater balance between your work and personal life.

ENTRY 9

Mind and Body Balance

"No man has the right to be an amateur in the matter of physical training. It is a shame for a man to grow old without seeing the beauty and strength of which his body is capable." - Socrates

The Stoics believed that the mind and body were interconnected, and that by taking care of our bodies through exercise, nutrition, and rest, we could improve our mental well-being as well. As busy Dads, it can be easy to prioritize our work and other responsibilities over our own health. However, neglecting our physical and mental health can lead to burnout, illness, and a decreased quality of life.

To achieve balance in this area, it is important to make time for regular exercise, healthy eating, and adequate sleep. Additionally, it is important to prioritize our mental health by seeking support when needed and engaging in self-care practices such as meditation, journaling, community, engaging in activities that bring us fulfillment, or a variety of healing treatments.

Our bodies are the vessels through which we experience the world, and maintaining our physical health is essential for our overall well-being. However, our mental health is just as important, and finding ways to nourish our minds can help us feel more balanced and grounded.

Having been a Calisthenics practitioner for many years I understand the body well, and it is through the practice of calisthenics that I found the minds power and the balance required for the two to become optimal.

Just like Stoicism, Calisthenics was another great concept made famous by the Greeks where it was used by athletes and soldiers to train for physical feats. The word "calisthenics" itself is derived from the Greek words "kalos," meaning beautiful, and "sthenos," meaning strength.

In many ways, calisthenics embodies the Stoic ideal of self-discipline and self-control. This aligns with the Stoic concept of focusing on what is within one's control.

Furthermore, calisthenics requires mental focus and concentration, another key tenet of Stoicism. By pushing oneself to complete a set of push-ups, for example, a person must train their mind to overcome physical discomfort and remain focused.

Calisthenics provides a physical expression of Stoic principles, encouraging individuals to develop self-discipline, mental fortitude, and a focus on internal strength rather than external circumstances.

It is the practice of using your own bodyweight to perform exercises, is a powerful tool for not only developing physical strength and endurance, but also for activating the mind. By engaging in bodyweight movements, individuals can improve their overall cognitive function and mental well-being.

Calisthenics is an excellent way to activate the mind because it requires a high level of focus and concentration. When performing bodyweight movements such as push-ups, pull-ups, and squats, the mind must be fully present and engaged in order to execute the movements with proper form and technique. This focus on the present moment helps to quiet the mind and promote a sense of mindfulness, which is essential for mental health and well-being.

In addition to promoting mindfulness, calisthenics can also help individuals develop a stronger mind-body connection. By performing movements that require the entire body to work in unison, individuals can develop a deeper sense of awareness and control over their physical selves. This increased awareness can lead to improved body posture, coordination, and balance, all of which contribute to overall physical and mental well-being.

Furthermore, calisthenics is an excellent way to promote overall physical fitness and health. By utilizing only one's own bodyweight, calisthenics can be performed anywhere and at any time, making it an incredibly convenient and accessible form of exercise. It also requires minimal equipment, making it a more cost-effective option compared to gym memberships or purchasing home gym equipment.

When it comes to calisthenics, the possibilities for exercises and movements are endless, allowing individuals to constantly challenge and push themselves. This constant challenge not only promotes physical growth and development, but also helps to build mental toughness and resilience. It is a powerful tool for improving both physical and mental health. By engaging in bodyweight movements, individuals can promote mindfulness, and develop a stronger mind-body connection.

WARRIOR ASSIGNMENT: Practice a daily calisthenics routine. Spend at least 15 minutes each day for a week practicing calisthenics, focusing on both the physical and mental aspects of the practice. Consider how you can bring balance into other areas of your life, such as work and relationships.

ENTRY 10

Material and Spiritual Balance

"Wealth consists not in having great possessions, but in having few wants." - Epictetus

The Stoics believed that we should strive to find a balance between material possessions and spiritual growth.

Our material possessions and achievements can bring us temporary pleasure and satisfaction, but they do not provide lasting fulfillment. By cultivating a sense of spirituality, whether through religion, nature, or personal beliefs, we can find a deeper sense of purpose and meaning in life.

This does not mean rejecting the material world altogether, but rather finding a healthy balance between material possessions and spiritual fulfillment. By valuing both aspects of life, we can find greater satisfaction and purpose in our daily lives, and we find those men with fewer needs in life were the wealthiest men of all.

In modern times, finding balance between our material and spiritual needs often involves navigating the tension between our desire for material possessions and our spiritual values and beliefs. To achieve balance in this area, it is important to prioritize our spiritual needs by cultivating practices that are mentioned constantly in these pages. Additionally, it is important to approach our material possessions with a sense of detachment and gratitude, recognizing that they are temporary and not the source of true happiness.

It is certainly a pleasure in having and earning material things, but detachment and gratitude towards them is a central concept in Stoic Alchemy. Stoics believe that while it is okay to enjoy material possessions, we should not be overly attached to them. Instead, we should recognize their impermanence and be grateful for what we have.

Detachment from material possessions means not being overly attached to them and not letting them define us. Instead, we should focus on what truly matters in life, such as our relationships, our values, and our personal growth. We should also recognise that material possessions can bring us pleasure and comfort, but they are not necessary for our happiness or well-being.

Gratitude as Stoic Warriors is something we will already be practicing, and we should also have gratitude towards our material possessions. We do this because we recognise the value that they bring to our lives. We should not take our possessions for granted, but instead, appreciate them and take care of them. We should also recognise that there are many people in the world who do not have the same material comforts that we do and be grateful for what we have.

When we are not attached to material possessions, we are less likely to be upset when we lose them or when they do not meet our expectations meaning we have less upset and negative occurrences in our lives. When we are grateful for what we have, we are less likely to be unhappy and more likely to appreciate the good things.

One famous Stoic quote on detachment and gratitude towards material possessions comes from Epictetus: "He is a wise man who does not grieve for the things which he has not, but rejoices for those which he has." This quote emphasizes the importance of gratitude towards what we have and the need to focus on what we do have rather than what we lack.

By recognizing the impermanence of material possessions and being grateful for what we have, we can lead a more peaceful and fulfilling life.

WARRIOR ASSIGNMENT: What material thing do you value most in your and what material thing do you use most in life? Find them and see if you can go a day, or a week without either. Find alternative methods and suggestions that may come from intuition to resolve any inconveniences that may occur by not having them.

Then go back to having them in your life and be grateful for their place and purpose in your life as you continue to use them.

ENTRY 11

Motion and Stillness

"Nature does not hurry, yet everything is accomplished." - Lao Tzu

Much like the masculine and feminine we need to know when to be active and when to go inside ourselves and find stillness. Much like the seasons we need our hibernation period to rest and recover, and in this we often find healing and answers to long lost questions w asked many moons ago.

In our fast-paced, constantly connected world, it can be easy to feel like we are always on the go, never stopping to take a breath. However, finding moments of stillness and quiet can be essential for our overall well-being.

This can involve practices such as meditation, yoga, or simply taking a few deep breaths throughout the day. By finding a balance between motion and stillness, we can cultivate a sense of calm and centeredness in our lives.

As busy Dads, we often find ourselves constantly on the go, striving to achieve our 'goals' and meet our responsibilities. However, it is important to recognize that rest and relaxation are equally important for our overall wellbeing and success, just as recovery days from training are the days where we do all our physical growth.

The Stoics recognized the importance of finding balance between activity and rest. They taught that a life of constant motion and activity could lead to burnout and exhaustion, while a life of constant rest and inactivity could lead to complacency and stagnation, and I must admit the latter is a demon of mine that I wrestle with daily, and in it I sometimes find myself moving and finding things to do which often results in me missing he benefit that come with comfort and regularity.

In modern times, finding balance between motion and stillness often means we are more drawn to one or the other, which again is a result of life conditioning and genetics. Creating the balance will either involve making time for rest and relaxation, even in the midst of a busy schedule, or getting up and finding activities and a purpose. The answer to both could involve engaging in hobbies or interests outside of work, taking regular breaks throughout the day, and making time for vacations or other forms of extended rest or activity.

When we engage in physical activity, we stimulate our body and mind, creating a surge of energy that can help us overcome stress and anxiety. However, it's important to balance this with moments of stillness, where we can focus on our breath and cultivate inner peace.

Meditation and mindfulness allow us to quiet the mind and turn our attention inward, helping us to better understand our thoughts, feelings, and emotions. By taking the time to cultivate stillness and mindfulness, we can become more aware of our physical and emotional needs, which can help us make better choices.

So, whether we are engaging in physical activity or practicing mindfulness and meditation, both are important for achieving balance in our lives. By combining movement with stillness, we can create a harmonious balance between the body and mind, allowing us to thrive.

WARROIR ASSIGNMENT: Pull together a practice that incorporates movement and stillness. A collaboration of working the body in a way that you enjoy with a mindful state exercise that allows for you to be still. This could look like Calisthenics followed with deep focus thought, or Martial Arts mixed with Chi gung, or Yoga followed by a calming breath session and meditation. For ideas or to follow a session download the Stoic Alchemist App in the app store or go to www.stoicalchemist.com.

ENTRY 12

Logic and Flow

"Logic will get you from A to B. Imagination will take you everywhere." - Albert Einstein

Without logical thinking and flow state there is no way this book could have come to be. Finding a sense of harmony between logic and flow is vital to a productive and forward flowing journey through life. Logic and reason are valuable tools for making sense of the world and solving problems, but they are not the only aspects of life. By embracing the flow of life, the spontaneous and unpredictable moments, we can find greater creativity and joy.

This can involve practices such as art, music, or simply allowing ourselves to be present in the moment without trying to control or analyse everything. By finding a balance between logic and flow, we can live a more dynamic life.

Balancing logic and flow involves recognising the importance of both rational thinking and intuitive wisdom in our lives. As busy men, we often rely on our logical minds to make decisions and solve problems. However, it is important to recognise that there is also value in tapping into our intuition and allowing ourselves to be guided by a sense of flow as the right answers usually come from this altered state and higher self.

The Stoics recognized the importance of both rational thinking and intuitive wisdom. They taught that logic and reason should be used to make sound decisions and assess situations, but also acknowledged that intuition and a sense of flow would guide us towards the right path.

In modern times, finding a balance between logic and flow often involves trusting our intuition and listening to our gut instincts, while also relying on our logical minds to make informed decisions. It may involve taking calculated risks, being open to new experiences, and allowing ourselves to be guided by a higher calling or voice.

The concept of the higher self has been around for centuries, but it's become more popular in recent years as people seek ways to tap into their full potential. The term "higher self" can sometimes be confusing, as it's often used interchangeably with the term "subconscious mind." However, the two are not quite the same, although they do share some similarities.

The higher self is often seen as the part of us that transcends the physical realm and is connected to something greater than ourselves. It's the part of us that has access to unlimited wisdom, creativity, and intuition. It's also the part of us that can guide us to our true purpose and help us reach our full potential.

On the other hand, the subconscious mind is the part of our mind that is not immediately available to our conscious awareness. It's the part of our mind that stores our beliefs, emotions, and memories, and it has a profound influence on our thoughts, feelings, and actions.

While the two concepts may seem different at first, they are in fact deeply interconnected. The subconscious mind is often seen as a bridge between the conscious mind and the higher self. By tapping into our subconscious mind through practices such as meditation and hypnosis, we can access the wisdom and intuition of our higher self.

Whether we choose to use the term "higher self" or "subconscious mind," the important thing is to recognise that we all have access to a deep well of wisdom and potential within us. By learning to tap into this inner wisdom, we can unlock our full potential and create a life that is aligned with our true purpose.

Connecting with the subconscious and higher self can be a powerful tool for personal growth and transformation. One effective way to do this is by using certain techniques such as geometry and gratitude. These techniques can activate both brain hemispheres, allowing for a deeper connection to the subconscious and higher self.

Geometry has long been used as a means of connecting to the spiritual and metaphysical realms. Sacred geometry, for example, is the use of specific patterns and shapes to tap into the deeper aspects of reality. These patterns and shapes can be found in nature and throughout the universe. By using these shapes and patterns in meditation or visualization practices, we can access the deeper aspects of ourselves and connect with the subconscious and higher self.

Gratitude as mentioned before is another powerful tool for connecting to the subconscious and higher self. By focusing on what we are thankful for, we shift our mindset from one of lack to one of abundance. This positive shift in mindset can activate the reward centre of the brain, releasing dopamine and other feel-good chemicals. These chemicals can increase motivation and help us stay focused on our goals. In addition, by expressing gratitude for what we already have, we attract more of what we desire into our lives.

The use of both geometry and gratitude can be a powerful combination in connecting to the subconscious and higher self. The right hemisphere of the brain, which is responsible for creativity and intuition, is activated by the visualization of the complex patterns and abundant thinking, while the left deals with the logic and complexities of the geometric shapes and the manifestation into reality.

Other techniques for connecting with the subconscious and higher self include meditation, visualisation, and dream journaling. These practices can help us access the deeper aspects of ourselves and gain insight into our true nature and purpose.

Like logic and flow we can take steps towards the balance of planning and creation which involves recognizing the importance of both structure and creativity in our lives. As men, we often rely on planning and structure to achieve our goals and meet our responsibilities. However, it is important to also recognize the value of creativity and innovation in achieving success.

The Stoics recognized the importance of both structure and creativity. They believed that structure and planning could help us achieve our goals, but also recognized the value of creative thinking and innovation in solving problems and achieving success.

In modern times, finding a balance between planning and creation often involves creating a structured plan or framework for achieving our goals, while also allowing room for creativity and innovation. This may involve brainstorming new ideas, experimenting with new approaches, and being open to new perspectives and insights.

So, warriors as we know we often find ourselves striving to achieve balance in our lives. We want to be successful in our careers, be present for our families, maintain our physical health, and find fulfilment in our spiritual and emotional lives. However, the reality is that achieving balance is not always easy, and we can easily find ourselves overcommitted and stretched too thin.

Hopefully with the information in this book and that assignments given we can start to find a balance that we can incorporate into our life's rituals.

We need balance in our masculine and feminine energies. While traditionally seen as opposite forces, both energies are necessary to live a well-rounded and fulfilling life. We need the strength and assertiveness of our masculine energy to tackle challenges and achieve goals, but we also need the nurturing and emotional awareness of our feminine energy to connect with others and understand our own emotions.

Finding balance also requires us to connect with nature and the rhythms of the world around us. We can do this by spending time in nature, getting regular exercise, and syncing our sleep patterns with the natural cycles of day and night. When we are in harmony with the world around us, we are better equipped to handle life's challenges and find inner peace.

Balance is crucial is in our relationship with material possessions. While it's important to have the things we need to live a comfortable life, we must not become too attached to material possessions or define our self-worth by them. Instead, we can practice gratitude for what we have and detach ourselves from the desire for more. This allows us to find contentment and fulfilment in life's simple pleasures and appreciate the people and experiences that truly matter.

The logical and creative aspects of our minds. We need the analytical and logical skills to problem-solve and make informed decisions, but we also need to tap into our creative flow to find inspiration and develop new ideas. By integrating both aspects of our minds, we can achieve anything in our lives.

Lastly, as dads, we need to balance our responsibilities as providers and caretakers with our own personal needs. It's important to be present for our families, but we must also take care of ourselves physically, emotionally, and spiritually. And with this I urge you to act on the assignments given, and use the simple solutions like exercise, meditation, and spending time with friends.

We are all busy, and can all think of excuses not to, or something more important, or less important if procrastination is the go-to…

Right, I'm going to break it down a moment, speak some truths, and crack some egos, even my own. Sometimes in life we fear our own potential. Sometimes we prefer the excuse, either because it's easier or it allows us to blame someone or something else for the reason we didn't 'get where we wanted'. But just know that as He-Man, our brilliant ambassador once said, 'You have the power'. So, use it, and everything that happens to you ultimately is in your hands!

So, without time for you, without implementing these strategies, you cannot be at your best, and without you at your best do those more important things really get the attention and concentration they deserve? Your family, your business, the world, and you deserve your best. So go live it!

It's an ongoing journey, and a hell of a slog, but one that is worth taking to live a truly magnificent life, and in the vein of balance, without the slog, and the sometimes-impenetrable hard times we would not be able to enjoy the times of peace and amazement with the same pure bliss.

GRAND WARRIOR ASSIGNMENT: Take some time to reflect on the areas of your life where you may be out of balance. Are there aspects of your life where you could cultivate more balance? What practices could you incorporate into your daily routine to help you find greater balance in life? This may involve a brainstorming session in which you can title the areas mentioned in the book and find activities and adventures that help bring you back into order!

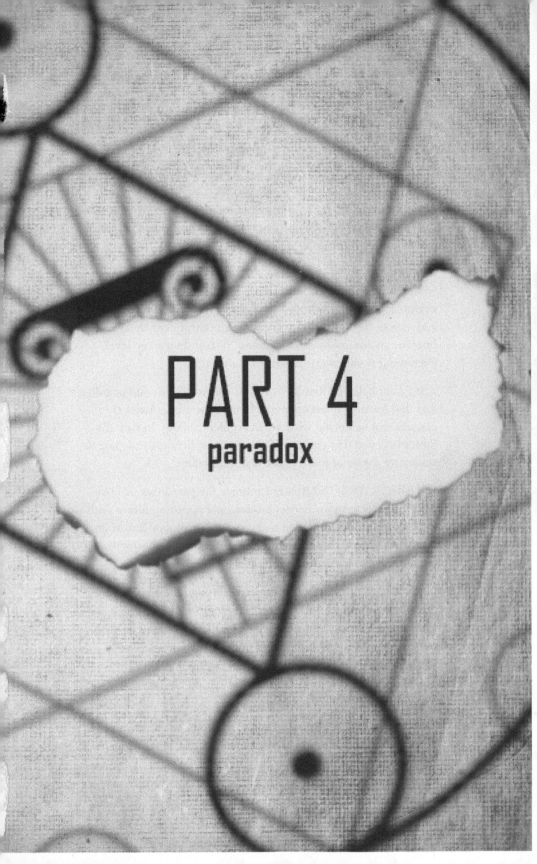

PART 4
paradox

ENTRY 13

Paradox

"Paradox is the pathway to truth. Through paradox, we transcend duality and discover the unity of opposites." - Deepak Chopra

Let us explore the concept of paradox, what it truly means, and how it relates to Stoic alchemy. Life is full of paradoxes, situations where two seemingly contradictory ideas can both be true. For example, the Stoics believed in the importance of both acceptance and action, recognising that we cannot control everything in life, but we can control how we respond to it, and on some level, everything is within our power to manifest.

The Stoics believed that life is full of contradictions and paradoxes, and that learning to accept and live with these paradoxes is essential for achieving wisdom and understanding. In fact, the Stoics believed that embracing these contradictions is the key to achieving a state of inner peace and tranquillity.

WARRIOR ASSIGNMENT: Embrace the paradoxes of life by exploring the tensions between seemingly opposing forces such as logic and intuition, planning and creation, or motion and stillness. Use these paradoxes as a tool for self-reflection and growth and cultivate a sense of openness and curiosity in your life.

One paradox that has been pondered through the ages is the relationship between individuality and interconnectedness. Embracing that Paradox can greatly reduce the deeper levels of anxiety that can be caused by the unknown complexities of existence, and in that intricate tapestry of existence, we find ourselves woven into a paradoxical dance between our individuality and interconnectedness.

On one hand, we are unique beings, with our own thoughts, beliefs, and experiences. On the other hand, we are undeniably interconnected, influencing, and being influenced by the world around us. Within this paradox lies a profound exploration of the human experience, delving into the realms of spirituality, belief systems, and the transformative power of our ideas and actions. Let us embark on a journey to understand the delicate balance between our individual selves and the vast web of connections that bind us together.

ENTRY 14

The Paradox of Individuality & Interconnectedness

"The universe is change; our life is what our thoughts make it." - Marcus Aurelius

As individuals, we are distinct manifestations of consciousness, each with our own perspectives, desires, and identities. Our thoughts, beliefs, and experiences shape our unique understanding of the world. We navigate life through the lens of our individuality, seeking personal growth, self-expression, and fulfilment This sense of separateness can be both empowering and limiting. It allows us to embrace our individuality, discover our unique gifts, and forge our own paths. However, it can also foster a sense of isolation, disconnection, and a longing to return to a greater sense of unity.

While our individual journeys are characterised by a sense of separation, we cannot ignore the profound interconnectedness that underlies our existence. Our actions ripple through the world, touching the lives of others in ways we may not always comprehend. Our individual choices and beliefs have the power to inspire, challenge, and transform the collective consciousness. We are not isolated islands but rather threads woven into the grand tapestry of humanity. Beyond this, through quantum physics and ancient spiritual beliefs, we find ourselves being informed that we are all energy, all source and all one.

Amidst the grand symphony of interconnectedness, the question arises: Why continue as individuals if we ultimately return to the source? The answer lies in the inherent purpose of individual expression. We are unique expressions of consciousness, imbued with our own perspectives, talents, and passions. Our individuality serves as a vehicle for self-discovery, growth, and the expression of our authentic essence.

The best analogy I have found is that if you look at the source (or energy) as the sea, we are but a cup of water taken out of that sea leading to our body obtaining the spirit. IF you further add a unique die or colouring to that cup of water that is then the soul, adding our unique purpose.

To me this means when we return to wherever we came from, when our cup gets emptied back into the sea, we add that little bit of colour that gives an essence of our individual 'us' back to the source, as through our individual journeys, we gain valuable experiences, learn profound lessons, and contribute to the collective expansion of consciousness. Each individual thread adds a unique flavour or colour to the grand tapestry of existence, enriching the overall fabric of life and adding tints of colour to the sea. Our continued individuality allows for the exploration of diverse perspectives, the cultivation of creativity, and the evolution of consciousness itself.

In exploring the paradox of interconnectedness, we encounter the profound notion that our lives are intertwined with the lives of others. Our thoughts, emotions, and actions reverberate through the collective consciousness, creating a ripple effect that extends far beyond our immediate sphere. We are connected to others not only by our shared experiences but also by the collective wisdom, beliefs, and aspirations that shape the human narrative.

While our individual paths may lead us back to the interconnected source, it is essential to recognize that this return is not a dissolution of our individuality but a profound integration. Just as the river merges with the vast ocean, we merge with the interconnectedness from which we sprang. In this dance of return and renewal, we expand our understanding of self and embrace a greater sense of unity.

As individuals, we carry with us the wisdom, experiences, and unique contributions gained during our journey. We bring these gifts back to the interconnected source, enriching it with our individual insights and perspectives. The cycle of individual expression and return allows for continuous growth, transformation, and the unfolding of a deeper understanding of the interconnected nature of existence.

In the paradoxical dance of individuality and interconnectedness, we discover the beauty and purpose of our existence. We continue as individuals, not in defiance of our interconnected nature, but to explore the vast spectrum of human experience. Our individuality allows us to fully express ourselves, create meaningful connections, and contribute to the collective evolution of consciousness.

Within the realm of interconnectedness, spiritual belief plays a significant role. No matter your beliefs, it is through our spiritual frameworks that we seek to make sense of the mysteries of life and our place within the cosmos. These belief systems offer guidance, solace, and a deeper understanding of our interconnected existence. Whether through religions, philosophical systems, or personal spiritual practices, we find a path to connect with something greater than ourselves.

Spiritual beliefs hold transformative power, as they shape our perception of reality and guide our actions. They provide a framework through which we cultivate compassion, empathy, and a sense of shared responsibility for the well-being of all beings. From an idea born in the depths of our spiritual exploration, we can spark movements, foster change, and contribute to the betterment of the world.

The paradox of individuality and interconnectedness is magnified when we recognize the profound impact our ideas and actions can have on the world. It is through our choices, big or small, that we contribute to the collective consciousness and shape the course of humanity. From a single act of kindness to the formulation of ground-breaking theories, our actions and ideas carry the potential to ignite change, challenge established norms, and inspire others to join in a shared vision of progress.

By embracing this paradox, we become conscious co-creators of our reality. We understand that our individuality does not exist in isolation but in relation to the interconnected web of existence. We recognize that our thoughts, beliefs, and actions can have far-reaching consequences, amplifying the transformative power of our shared human experience.

In the intricate dance of individuality and interconnectedness, we discover the essence of our existence. We are both unique beings, navigating life through the lens of our individual perspectives, and interconnected threads, shaping and being shaped by the collective consciousness. It is by embracing these paradoxes and recognizing their complexity, we can cultivate a deeper sense of wisdom and understanding in life. Rather than seeking simplistic answers or black-and-white thinking, we can embrace the nuances and complexities of life, and often give compassion and understanding to opposing opinions.

At the core of this paradox lies a deep truth: our individuality is not separate from the interconnected whole; it is an integral part of it. Just as the diverse colours and shapes in a mosaic contribute to its overall beauty, our unique expressions of self-enrich the fabric of existence. Each individual is like a unique brushstroke in a grand masterpiece, adding depth, texture, and vibrancy.

Through our individual journeys, we embark on a path of self-discovery and growth. We learn to navigate the challenges and embrace the joys that life presents. We develop resilience, compassion, and wisdom, all of which become part of the collective wisdom of humanity. Our individual experiences become stories that inspire, lessons that guide, and insights that transform.

As we navigate the paradox of individuality and interconnectedness, it is crucial to remember that both aspects are essential for our personal and collective evolution. We are called to honour our individuality while cultivating a deep sense of empathy and interconnectedness. We find balance by recognising that our individual journey is not isolated but deeply intertwined with the journeys of others.

So, let us celebrate our individuality, nurture our unique gifts, and embark on the journey of self-discovery. Let us also recognise the interconnectedness that binds us all, encouraging compassion, collaboration, and a sense of shared responsibility for the well-being of all beings. In this dance of paradox, we find the beauty of being both individuals and interconnected souls on the wondrous tapestry of existence.

WARRIOR ASSIGNMENT: Embrace the paradoxical elements of your life by exploring the tensions between your personal and professional journey, your inner and outer selves, or your spiritual and material aspirations. Use these paradoxes as a tool for personal transformation and growth.

ENTRY 15

Paradox of perception

"Everything we hear is an opinion, not a fact. Everything we see is a perspective, not the truth." - Marcus Aurelius

The 'Theory of Everything' has been a subject of debate among scientists and philosophers for centuries. It refers to a single, unified explanation for all the phenomena in the universe, including the laws of physics, the behaviour of matter and energy, and the nature of time and space.

However, I have a theory that the idea of a 'Theory of Everything' is a paradox. Why? Because everything is subjective. Our perceptions and experiences shape how we understand and interpret the world around us. What may seem logical and true to one person may not hold the same weight for someone else.

This paradox is reflected in the duality of our existence - light and dark, yin and yang, masculine and feminine, logical, and creative. These opposites are not separate entities, but rather two sides of the same coin. They exist in a delicate balance, and it is through the interplay of these opposites that we find meaning and purpose in our lives.

In the same way, our understanding of the universe and its laws is subjective. Our theories and explanations are limited by our current understanding and the tools we have available to explore and observe the world. As we continue to advance and develop new technologies and techniques for exploring the universe, our theories and explanations may evolve and change, but as ever, still being limited by our own creations and human intelligence to understand it.

However, this does not mean that we should dismiss the idea of a Theory of Everything altogether. Rather, we should recognize that our understanding of the universe is constantly evolving and expanding, and that any theory we develop is subject to change and revision as we gain new knowledge and insights.

In the end, the pursuit of a Theory of Everything may be less about finding a single, definitive explanation for the universe, and more about embracing the paradoxical nature of our existence and recognizing that our understanding of the world is always subjective and limited. By embracing this paradox, we can cultivate a deeper sense of curiosity, wonder, and appreciation for the mysteries of the universe.

Further, subjectivity is an intrinsic aspect of the human experience. We perceive and interpret the world through the lens of our individual perspectives, shaped by our unique backgrounds, beliefs, and biases. Even when dealing with matters that seem objective, such as scientific theories or empirical data, our perception and understanding are inherently subjective.

Consider scientific theories, for instance. They are built upon rigorous observations, experimentation, and analysis. They strive to provide explanations that are consistent, reliable, and universally applicable. However, the interpretation and acceptance of these theories can vary among individuals. One person may embrace a theory wholeheartedly, while another may scrutinise it or propose alternative explanations. This divergence arises from the subjectivity inherent in how we interpret and make sense of the evidence presented to us.

Our perception of reality is shaped by our subjective filters and cognitive processes. We selectively attend to certain aspects of our environment, influenced by our interests, values, and emotional states. Our minds actively construct our experience, filtering and interpreting information based on pre-existing beliefs and mental models. What one person perceives as an objective reality may be significantly different from another's perception of the same situation.

Even when it comes to matters of fact, our subjective biases can come into play. Confirmation bias, for instance, leads us to seek and interpret information that confirms our pre-existing beliefs, while downplaying contradictory evidence. This bias can affect our perception of reality and alter our ability to objectively evaluate information. There for to be able to navigate this reality, paradoxically we must acknowledge general consensus on the majority of objective understandings. For example, 'I am sitting on a chai' or at least I think I am! So, is objectivity just a majority vote on multiple human consciousness' current reality?

Recognising the subjectivity inherent in our perceptions and interpretations can be both humbling and liberating. It reminds us that our understanding of the world is limited and that there may be multiple valid perspectives. It encourages us to approach knowledge with intellectual humility, open-mindedness, and a willingness to consider alternative viewpoints.

Embracing the subjectivity of our experiences does not mean abandoning objectivity altogether. It means acknowledging that our perception and interpretation are inherently filtered through subjective lenses. It calls for a constant evaluation of our own biases, a commitment to critical thinking, and an openness to revising our beliefs in light of new evidence, but also in trusting our intuition.

In summary, the paradox of subjectivity and objectivity arises from the understanding that our individual perceptions and interpretations are inherently subjective, while also recognising the interconnectedness of all beings at a fundamental level. On one hand, our subjective experiences and perspectives shape how we perceive and interpret the world, making objectivity seemingly elusive. On the other hand, the notion that we are all interconnected and derive from a common source challenges the boundaries of individual subjectivity.

The paradox lies in reconciling these two perspectives. While subjectivity suggests that our experiences and interpretations are unique to us, the understanding of interconnectedness reminds us that we are all interconnected and share a common essence. This realisation blurs the boundaries between subject and object, self and other, and challenges the notion of individuality.

From this perspective, the subjective-objective argument becomes a paradox, as the subjective nature of our experiences seems to contradict the interconnectedness that unifies us all. It highlights the limitations of purely subjective or purely objective perspectives and calls for a deeper exploration of the complex relationship between the two.

Rather than seeking a definitive resolution to this paradox, it invites us to embrace the tension and ambiguity that it presents. It encourages us to recognise the subjective nature of our experiences while also acknowledging the interconnectedness that binds us together. It invites us to hold space for both perspectives, appreciating the uniqueness of individual perspectives while recognizing the underlying unity that transcends them.

Navigating this paradox requires us to cultivate awareness, humility, and an open-mindedness to different ways of perceiving and understanding the world. It challenges us to embrace the mystery and complexity of existence, recognizing that our understanding is always limited and evolving. Even in my writing you will hear bias and subjective opinion to my beliefs and morals, but if you have come this far then there are definitely areas that you resonate with and that align with your own, but ultimately it is up to you to create your own subjective understanding on these words.

Ultimately, understanding the subjectivity of our perceptions can encourage empathy, compassion, and intellectual growth while reminding us that others may hold valid perspectives and that there is value in engaging in dialogue and seeking common ground. By recognizing and appreciating the interplay between subjectivity and objectivity, we can navigate the complexities of our world with greater wisdom and understanding. It invites us to transcend binary thinking and embrace the richness of multiple perspectives. It reminds us of the inherent mystery and wonder of existence, inviting us to explore the depths of our subjective experiences while honouring the interconnected fabric that binds us all.

WARRIOR ASSIGNMENT: Take some time to reflect on the paradoxical elements of your life. Are there areas where you may be seeking simplistic answers or avoiding the complexities of a situation? Look from above the situation and oppose every thought or opinion of your own with a contradictory subjective opinion learning how can you embrace the paradoxes in your life and cultivate a deeper sense of wisdom and understanding?

ENTRY 16

The Paradox of control

"The chief task in life is simply this: to identify and separate matters so that I can say clearly to myself which are externals not under my control, and which have to do with the choices I actually control." - Epictetus

Another of the paradoxes that the Stoics often spoke about is the paradox of control. On the one hand, the Stoics believed that we have complete control over our thoughts and attitudes, often going deeper into the matter of frequency control, visualisation, manifestation, and inner change. We can choose how we respond to any situation, and we can choose to see challenges and obstacles as opportunities for growth and transformation. On the other hand, some Stoics recognised that there are many things in life that are outside of our control, such as the actions of other people, the weather, or even our own bodies.

In our quest for personal growth, we often find ourselves seeking control. Control over our circumstances, control over our emotions, and control over the outcomes we desire. We believe that by exerting control, we can shape our lives according to our will and manifest our desires into reality. However, the paradox lies in the recognition that some things are beyond our control, and the more we grasp for control, the more elusive it becomes. As with everything at the other extreme is surrender without compromise, this often results in a lack of personal morals and can result in a self-destruct state of mind. As within the area of balance, we find the best state in a place where we can surrender and accept, but also assess and bring the letting go into an actionable state of being.

One of the areas where this paradox becomes evident is in our emotions. We often strive to control our emotional states, believing that we should always be happy, positive, and in control of our feelings. However, the more we resist and try to control our emotions, the more they seem to persist and intensify. It is in surrendering to our emotions, allowing them to be felt and acknowledged, that we find a sense of peace and release.

The paradox of control teaches us that true control lies in our ability to let go and surrender. It is not about suppressing or denying our emotions but rather embracing them with compassion and understanding. By acknowledging the full spectrum of our emotions and allowing them to flow, we create space for healing and growth.

To look into the belief and science of raising our vibrations or frequencies, allows us to understand that there is a lot to life that is within our control, and due to our current frequency we find ourselves in our current situation, good or bad. This idea suggests that by elevating our energetic state, we can attract more positive experiences into our lives. It involves consciously choosing thoughts, emotions, and actions that align with higher states of being such as love, joy, and gratitude.

However, the paradox arises when we realize that the very act of striving to raise our vibrations can create resistance and attachment, thus inhibiting our progress. It is in the surrendering of the need to control our vibrations that we actually allow them to naturally rise. Rather than forcefully trying to change our frequency, we can cultivate an attitude of openness and receptivity, allowing the natural flow of energy within us. This opens and allows for us to access the areas of manifestation. Manifestation suggests that by aligning our thoughts, beliefs, and intentions with the desired outcomes, we can attract them into our lives. However, the paradox lies in recognising that while we have the power to co-create our reality, we are also part of a larger, interconnected web of existence that operates beyond our individual control. It is here that we find out that manifestation starts with gratitude for what you have already brought to be, and in bringing good intentions in for others.

In practicing manifestation, we must learn to strike a balance between taking inspired action towards our desired journey and surrendering to the unfolding of life. It is about setting intentions, visualising our desired outcomes, and taking aligned action, while also trusting in the wisdom of the universe and being open to unexpected possibilities.

WARRIOR ASSIGNEMNT: Visualising and Raising Frequency, follow the steps.

To engage with the paradox of control and explore the power of visualisation and frequency raising, you can incorporate the following practice into your daily routine:

1. Find a quiet and comfortable space where you can relax and be free from distractions.

2. Begin by focusing on your breath, allowing yourself to enter a state of calm and relaxation.

3. Visualize yourself in a situation or experience that aligns with your highest vision of yourself. See the details, feel the emotions, and engage all your senses as if it were happening in the present moment. Feeling is the key! If you can open your heart to the situation and align you emotions with the vision what you need will come to pass.

4. As you immerse yourself in the visualisation, bring awareness to your energetic state. Notice any sensations, emotions, or thoughts that arise within you, don't dismiss, or try to rid any thoughts, allow them to be, and with no answer let them pass or stay.

5. If you find yourself feeling any resistance or attachment to the outcome, gently let go and surrender to the process. Trust that the moment has your best interests at heart.

6. After completing the visualisation, take a few moments to reflect on the experience. Notice any shifts in your energy, emotions, or perspective. Acknowledge any insights or intuitive guidance that may have arisen during the practice.

Now, let's delve deeper into the practice of raising your frequency. Frequency refers to the vibrational energy emitted by every living being and object. It is influenced by our thoughts, emotions, beliefs, and actions. By consciously raising our frequency, we can elevate our state of being and attract experiences that resonate with our higher selves.

As mentioned, one powerful way to raise your frequency is through the cultivation of gratitude. Gratitude is a transformative practice that shifts our focus from lack to abundance, from complaints to appreciation. Take a few moments each day to express gratitude for the blessings in your life. It could be as simple as appreciating the warmth of the sun on your skin, the love of your family, or the opportunities for growth and learning.

Engaging in acts of kindness and compassion is another way to raise your frequency. By extending love and support to others, you tap into the interconnectedness of all beings. Perform random acts of kindness, volunteer your time for a cause you believe in, or simply offer a listening ear to someone in need. As you give, you also receive, creating a positive ripple effect in your own life and the lives of others.

Practicing mindfulness and presence is essential in raising your frequency. When you bring your attention to the present moment, you free yourself from the worries of the past and anxieties about the future. Engage in activities that promote mindfulness, such as meditation, deep breathing exercises, or mindful movement practices like yoga or tai chi. These practices help you cultivate inner stillness and align with the natural flow of life.

And to hammer it home, nurturing a connection with nature can be a profound way to raise your frequency. Spend time outdoors, immerse yourself in the beauty of the natural world, and attune yourself to the rhythms of the earth. Nature has a way of grounding us, reminding us of our inherent connection to all living things. Find solace in the serenity of a forest, the vastness of the ocean, or the vibrant colours of a sunset. Allow yourself to be present and open to the wisdom that nature holds.

Remember, the paradox of control lies in the understanding that while we have the power to shape our lives, we are also part of a larger, interconnected whole. Embrace the journey of personal growth and self-discovery but do so with a sense of surrender and openness. Allow yourself to flow with the currents of life, trusting that everything unfolds in perfect timing and accordance with the greater plan.

By incorporating these practices into your daily life, you can actively participate in the process of raising your frequency, aligning with your higher self, and inviting positive transformation into your life. Embrace the paradox, embrace the interconnectedness, and embark on a journey of self-discovery and growth that transcends the limitations of the mind and connects you to the vastness of your soul.

Our Stoic friends had a more material view that resonates with this in the idea that we should focus on what is within our control and let go of what is outside of our control. This means that we should focus on our own thoughts, attitudes, and behaviours, and not worry about things such as the actions of other people or the weather. By focusing on what is within our control, we can achieve a sense of inner peace.

And to delve in to the context of paradox, this means that we should embrace the paradoxes of life and see them as opportunities for growth and transformation that are happening in line with our highest purpose. We should not try to eliminate paradoxes or contradictions, but rather learn to accept and live with them. By doing so, we can achieve a greater sense of wisdom and understanding and develop a more balanced life.

ENTRY 17

Paradox of pleasure & pain

"He who indulges in empty pleasure is like a man who hunts for game in a swamp, and finds nothing but slime and mire." - Seneca

Life is a dance of contrasts, where pleasure and pain intertwine in a never-ending paradox. In our pursuit of happiness, we often seek pleasure and avoid pain, believing that one can exist without the other. But the truth is, they are inseparable companions on our journey through existence. To become a Stoic Alchemist, one must learn to navigate this paradox and find wisdom and growth in its midst of the pain.

The Stoic Alchemist, an embodiment of the principles we have explored in this book, is not immune to the pleasures and pains of life. Instead, this archetype embraces the dynamic interplay between these opposing forces, recognizing their inherent connection and the lessons they offer.

Pleasure, in its various forms, can be a source of joy, fulfillment, and inspiration. It can arise from the simplest of experiences, like savouring a delicious meal, witnessing a breath-taking sunset, or sharing a heartfelt connection with a loved one. Pleasure uplifts our spirits, ignites our passions, and nourishes our souls.

Yet, the pursuit of pleasure alone can lead to a shallow and fleeting existence. It can blind us to the realities of life, create attachments that bind us, and cloud our judgment. Excessive pursuit of pleasure can also lead to hedonism, where we become slaves to our desires, seeking immediate gratification without considering the consequences. This is relevant in current society where peoples attention span gets shorter and shorter and the world loses its gratitude for a piece of heartfelt content in less than a few seconds, only to swipe to the next one.

On the other hand, pain is an inevitable part of the human experience. It encompasses physical discomfort, emotional turmoil, and the challenges that life presents. Pain tests our resilience, evokes our deepest emotions, and provides opportunities for growth and transformation. It is through pain that we learn resilience, empathy, and the true value of joy. Yet, just as excessive pursuit of pleasure can be detrimental, so too can an aversion to pain. Avoidance of pain can lead to stagnation, fear, and a life lived in the shadows. By rejecting pain, we deny ourselves the opportunity to learn, evolve, and discover our true strength.

In this, we find the power of hormesis. With hormesis, we learn the relationship between pain and growth. It seems counterintuitive that subjecting ourselves to discomfort and challenges, but this surrender can actually lead to positive outcomes. Hormesis is an ancient principle that has been recognised by various cultures throughout history and used extensively in sciences and anti-venom research.

Pain is often viewed as something to be avoided, a signal of danger or harm. It triggers our natural instinct to protect ourselves and seek comfort. However, the paradox lies in the fact that pain, when experienced in measured doses, can be transformative. It can be the catalyst for growth, both physically and mentally. The Stoics recognized this paradox and understood that pain can serve as a powerful teacher, guiding us towards greater strength and wisdom.

Hormesis is a concept rooted in ancient wisdom, dating back to the teachings of Hippocrates and Paracelsus. It is the idea that exposure to low to moderate levels of stress or discomfort can stimulate adaptive responses in our bodies and minds. Just as a muscle needs resistance to grow stronger, our minds and bodies require challenges to develop resilience and adaptability.

Hormesis operates on the principle of "what doesn't kill you makes you stronger." When we intentionally expose ourselves to controlled amounts of stress or discomfort, our bodies and minds respond by adapting and becoming more resilient. Physical exercise is a prime example of hormesis in action. When we push ourselves to our limits during a workout, our muscles break down, triggering a healing response that results in stronger, more capable bodies.

Similarly, in the realm of personal development, embracing discomfort and challenges can lead to profound growth and transformation.

Embracing hormesis requires finding the delicate balance between pushing ourselves and allowing for rest and recovery. It is not about subjecting ourselves to constant pain or discomfort, but rather about incorporating intentional periods of challenge and growth into our lives. This could mean setting goals that stretch our abilities, taking on new projects or responsibilities, or engaging in practices that push us out of our comfort zones. By doing so, we create opportunities for growth, honing our skills, expanding our perspectives, and cultivating resilience.

WARRIOR ASSIGNMENT: To harness the power of hormesis in your own life, identify an area of your life where you have been avoiding discomfort or challenges. It could be a skill you've been hesitant to pursue, a difficult conversation you've been avoiding, or a project that scares you. Commit to taking a small step towards embracing that discomfort. Start with a manageable challenge, something that pushes you just beyond your comfort zone but is within reach. As you progress, gradually increase the level of difficulty.

Throughout this process, pay attention to how embracing discomfort impacts your growth and resilience. Notice the shifts in your mindset, the newfound confidence, and the expanded capacity to handle adversity. Embrace the paradox that lies within the pain, knowing that it holds the potential for your personal transformation and inherent joy in all aspects of life.

In our quest for optimal health and resilience, we often seek out methods that can push our bodies and minds to adapt and grow stronger. Two powerful tools that have gained significant attention in recent years are fasting and cold exposure. These practices harness the principle of hormesis, utilising controlled doses of stress to elicit numerous health benefits.

Fasting is the intentional abstention from food for a defined period. The methods of fasting have been practiced by various cultures and religions throughout history. Beyond its spiritual significance, fasting offers remarkable physiological benefits. One of the key effects is the induction of autophagy. Autophagy has been linked to improved longevity, reduced inflammation, and enhanced cellular health. Additionally, fasting triggers a surge in human growth hormone (HGH), which aids in muscle growth, fat burning, and overall rejuvenation.

Autophagy is a cellular process that removes damaged or dysfunctional components within cells. During fasting, when the body is in a state of energy deprivation, it turns to its own cellular components for fuel. This process triggers autophagy, allowing the body to recycle and eliminate damaged proteins and organelles. By clearing out these cellular waste products, autophagy promotes cellular renewal, improving overall cellular health and longevity.

Human growth hormone (HGH) is a hormone that plays a crucial role in growth, metabolism, and tissue repair. HGH promotes muscle growth, accelerates fat burning, and enhances collagen synthesis, leading to improved skin elasticity and reduced signs of aging. By incorporating regular fasting periods into your routine, you can tap into the potential of HGH and harness its rejuvenating effects.

The practice can be incorporated in short or long stints, and there is a right and a lot of very wrong ways to incorporate fasting into your lifestyle. Current studies show that autophagy begins at around twenty-four hours of fasting and although there are many benefits to intermittent fasting such as glycogen balancing the blood sugars, the studies suggest that a beneficial fast can be anywhere between sixteen and thirty-six hours. However, the act of fasting and its benefits are individual, it is not suggested for people who have any medical conditions or physical and psychological issues.

Cold exposure, such as cold showers, ice baths, or outdoor cold exposure, is another potent hormetic stressor with numerous benefits. When subjected to cold temperatures, our bodies activate a process called cold-induced thermogenesis, which boosts metabolism and increases energy expenditure. Cold exposure has been shown to improve circulation, strengthen the immune system, and increase resilience to stress. It can also enhance mental clarity, focus, and mood by activating the release of endorphins and neurotransmitters like dopamine and serotonin.

Both fasting and cold exposure play a significant role in enhancing immune function. Fasting promotes the renewal of immune cells and can reduce the risk of chronic diseases by improving immune surveillance. Cold exposure, on the other hand, activates the production of white blood cells, increasing their ability to fight off infections. When combined, these practices create a powerful synergy that bolsters the immune system, providing a robust defence against pathogens and supporting overall health.

It is essential to approach fasting and cold exposure with caution and respect for individual limits. Beginners should start with shorter fasting windows and gradually increase the duration as their bodies adapt. Similarly, cold exposure should be introduced gradually, allowing the body to acclimate to lower temperatures. Safety precautions, such as consulting a healthcare professional and practicing in a controlled environment are crucial to prevent possible injury to self.

WARRIOR ASSIGNMENT: To incorporate the benefits of fasting and cold exposure into your life, I encourage you to embark on a personal exploration. Begin by implementing intermittent fasting, gradually extending the fasting window based on your comfort level and personal journey. Experiment with cold exposure, starting with short cold showers and gradually working your way up to longer exposure or ice baths. Take note of how these practices make you feel, both physically and mentally, and observe any positive changes in your energy, mood, and overall well-being.

Fasting and cold exposure are powerful tools rooted in the principle of hormesis, offering numerous health benefits for both mind and body. By harnessing the effects of autophagy, HGH release, improved immunity, and increased resilience, these practices can optimise your health, enhance your longevity, and deepen your understanding of the incredible capabilities of the human body. As you embark on this journey of hormesis, remember to listen to your body, practice safely, and embrace the transformative power of these ancient practices.

Note: It is important to consult with a healthcare professional before implementing any significant changes to your diet or lifestyle, especially if you have any underlying health conditions. Additionally, it is essential to approach fasting and cold exposure with moderation and respect for your individual limits.

WARRIOR ASSIGNMENT: Find a quiet space where you can relax and visualise the positive impact these practices will have on your body, mind, and overall well-being. Envision yourself feeling energised, resilient, and in optimal health. Alongside visualisation, practice raising your frequency by engaging in activities that bring you joy. Notice how these practices shift your outlook and enhance your overall frequency and work on your beliefs behind the benefits.

The Stoic Alchemist recognises that pleasure and pain are intertwined aspects of our existence, and that the key lies in our response to them. They cultivate an attitude of equanimity, acknowledging the transient nature of both pleasure and pain. They embrace pleasure with gratitude and savour each moment in the knowledge of its impermanent. They also meet pain with acceptance, resilience, and a commitment to grow stronger through adversity. The true interpretation of 'Cheerfulness in the face of adversity'!

Embrace the dance of pleasure and pain, for within it lies the wisdom of the Stoic Alchemist. By embracing this paradox, we transcend the limitations of a pleasure-centric existence and open ourselves to a deeper and more meaningful engagement with life.

The paradox of pleasure and pain invites us to embrace the full spectrum of human experience. As Stoic Alchemists, we learn to navigate this dance, finding wisdom, growth, and resilience in both pleasure and pain. By cultivating gratitude, acceptance, and mindful awareness, we unlock the transformative power of this paradox, allowing us to live fully, authentically, and with a profound understanding of life's intricate tapestry.

Embrace the paradox, and let it guide you on the path of the Stoic Alchemist.

Stoicism focuses on principles such as virtue, acceptance of the present moment, and the understanding that external circumstances are beyond our control. However, the concept of embracing the paradox of pleasure and pain aligns with Stoic philosophy by encouraging a balanced and mindful approach to life.

The Stoic Alchemist, as an archetype, embodies the principles of Stoicism and applies them to the paradox of pleasure and pain. This archetype recognizes that pleasure and pain are natural and unavoidable aspects of life. Instead of clinging to pleasure or avoiding pain, the Stoic Alchemist learns to find contentment and equanimity in both states.

Through the practice of mindfulness and self-awareness, the Stoic Alchemist cultivates an inner resilience that allows them to navigate the fluctuations of pleasure and pain with grace. They understand that pleasure is fleeting and impermanent, and they do not become overly attached to it. Likewise, when faced with pain, they approach it with acceptance and use it as an opportunity for growth and self-improvement.

The Stoic Alchemist also recognises that the pursuit of pleasure for its own sake can lead to a shallow and unsatisfying life. By acknowledging the interconnection between pleasure and pain, they develop a deeper understanding of the inherent impermanence of all things. This understanding frees them from excessive desires and allows them to find contentment in the present moment, regardless of external circumstances.

In acceptance of the pleasure and pain paradox, the Stoic Alchemist demonstrates the ability to find joy and fulfillment in the simplest of experiences. They find beauty in the ordinary, appreciate the small pleasures of life, and derive satisfaction from acts of kindness and virtue. By embracing the inevitability of pain, they are able to face adversity with courage and resilience, knowing that it is a necessary part of the human experience.

So, as you embark on your journey to embody the principles of the Stoic Alchemist, I invite you to contemplate the paradox of pleasure and pain in your own life. Reflect on how you approach pleasure and whether it becomes a source of attachment or dissatisfaction. Explore how you respond to pain and whether you view it as an opportunity for growth or a source of suffering.

Warrior Assignment: I encourage you to practice gratitude and mindfulness in your daily life. Take a few moments each day to reflect on the simple pleasures you encounter and express gratitude for them. Similarly, when faced with moments of discomfort or pain, approach them with acceptance and a willingness to learn from them. Observe how this practice transforms your relationship with pleasure and pain, allowing you to navigate the paradox with greater equanimity and wisdom.

Remember, the paradox of pleasure and pain is not about denying ourselves joy or seeking unnecessary suffering. It is about finding balance, embracing the ebb and flow of life, and cultivating a deeper understanding of ourselves and the world around us.

In the footsteps of the Stoic Alchemist, let us embark on this journey of self-discovery, embracing the paradox of pleasure and pain, and unlocking the transformative power it holds.

WARRIOR ASSIGNMENT: Embrace the uncertainty and ambiguity of life by learning to live with paradox and contradiction. Recognise that life is inherently unpredictable and that the only constant is change and use this awareness as a tool for growth and transformation.

83

ENTRY 18

Paradox of fate & freewill

"God has given you a mind capable of reflection and a will that is subject to no compulsion; he has made you your own master and given you the power to shape your own life. That is the greatest gift he has bestowed upon you. You can be happy, no matter what the external circumstances may be, if you have the right attitude of mind." - Epictetus

Fate, Free Will, and the Alchemy of Life's Paths

In the journey of life, we often find ourselves grappling with the paradoxical nature of fate and free will. On one hand, it seems that our lives are guided by a predetermined course, influenced by external forces beyond our control. On the other hand, we possess the agency to make choices and shape our destinies. This paradox lies at the heart of the Stoic Alchemist's contemplation, intertwining Stoic beliefs with the rich philosophy of the Japanese four life paths: Tenmei, Shukumei, Unmei, and Shimei. In this exploration, we will delve into the essence of this paradox, examining the Stoic perspective while embracing the multifaceted nature of our existence.

The Stoics believed in the concept of fate, known as "hegemonikon," or the ruling faculty of the mind. According to Stoic teachings, fate encompasses the circumstances and events that befall us, shaped by a divine order governing the universe. They believed that certain aspects of our lives were predetermined, beyond our immediate control. However, Stoicism emphasised that our response to these external events is within our power, giving rise to the notion of free will as a means of navigating the world.

Despite our capacity for free will, the Stoic Alchemists acknowledged the inherent limitations of human agency. They recognised that our control over external events is often illusory, as countless variables influence the outcomes of our actions. This recognition humbles us and encourages us to focus on what lies within our sphere of influence our thoughts, attitudes, and responses – rather than becoming consumed by the pursuit of control over external circumstances. Although there is also the theory that in focusing on our own attitudes and responses, we can ultimately influence anything external if only we knew the innate power that lies within and connects us all to everything, or maybe it is the understanding that everything external is a projection of our internal reality that will give us ultimate control over our life journey. This understanding may just be the secret to give us the power to navigate our journey to our desires, but ultimately, only if it is to bring the highest balance to all the people and energies around us.

A further thought train is one I love to contemplate as it is from the country where my heart lies, and that is in the realm of Japanese philosophy. It is 'the four life paths' – Tenmei, Shukumei, Unmei, and Shimei. These four life paths offer an insightful perspective on the interplay between fate and free will. Each path represents a distinct approach to life, reflecting the diverse experiences and choices we encounter.

Tenmei: The Path of Heavenly Decree:

Tenmei encompasses the belief that certain aspects of our lives are predetermined by a higher power or cosmic forces. It highlights the acceptance of events beyond our control and encourages embracing the lessons and growth opportunities that arise from them.

By embracing the principles of Tenmei, we learn to surrender to the larger forces at play in our lives and find peace in accepting what is beyond our control. This allows us to cultivate humility and a deep trust in the unfolding of life's journey.

Shukumei: The Path of Personal Effort:

Shukumei emphasises the role of personal effort and the choices we make in shaping our destiny. It recognises the importance of taking responsibility for our actions, diligently working towards our goals, and persevering in the face of challenges.

Shukumei reminds us of our personal responsibility and the power of our choices. By taking ownership of our actions and decisions, we become conscious co-creators of our destiny, aligning our lives with our values and principles.

Unmei: The Path of Destiny:

Unmei represents the convergence of external circumstances and personal choices. It suggests that while certain events may be destined, our responses and actions within those situations can influence the ultimate outcome. Unmei encourages an attitude of adaptability and resourcefulness in navigating the twists and turns of life.

Unmei teaches us to adapt and flow with the ever-changing circumstances of life. Through resilience and flexibility, we find strength in navigating challenges and discovering opportunities within adversity.

Shimei: The Path of Personal Mission:

Shimei embodies the notion that each individual has a unique purpose or mission in life. It emphasises the pursuit of one's true calling, aligning actions and choices with a deeper sense of meaning and contribution to the world.

Shimei calls us to uncover our unique purpose and contribute to the greater good. By living with intention and dedicating ourselves to a meaningful mission, we find fulfilment and make a positive impact on the world around us.

By integrating the wisdom of these four life paths, we embark on a transformative journey of self-discovery, personal growth, and spiritual alchemy. We embrace the paradoxes of life, recognising that if our beliefs lead us to a sense of fate or happenstance where we believe aspects of our journey are beyond our control, then we have the power to shape our responses and cultivate inner harmony.

Through the practices of Stoic philosophy, mindfulness, self-reflection, and the application of alchemical principles, we unlock the potential within ourselves to transmute challenges into opportunities, transform our perception of reality, and live a life of purpose and fulfilment.

In the realm of the Stoic Alchemist, the paradox of fate and free will takes on a transformative meaning. Rather than viewing fate and free will as opposing forces, the Stoic Alchemists recognise their interdependence. They understand that while certain aspects of our lives are subject to external influences and predetermined events, our inner disposition and choices play a vital role in shaping our experiences and perceptions of those events.

By embracing this paradox, we transcend the binary notion of either complete control or complete surrender to fate. Instead, we cultivate a mindset of harmony and alignment with the unfolding of life. We recognise that while there may be a belief of the inability to control every external circumstance, we possess the power to control our inner responses and the way we navigate the challenges that come our way.

At the core of the Stoic Alchemist's journey is the alchemy of perception and choice. Through the practice of mindfulness and self-awareness, we learn to observe our thoughts and emotions without becoming enslaved by them. We cultivate the ability to choose our responses consciously, aligning them with our values and principles.

This transformative process allows us to transmute the raw materials of fate and free will into wisdom and virtue. We develop resilience in the face of adversity, embracing the lessons and growth opportunities that arise from challenging situations. We also learn to appreciate and cherish the moments of joy and abundance, recognising their transient nature and savouring them fully.

The paradox of fate and free will lies at the heart of the Stoic Alchemist's journey. Through the integration of Stoic beliefs and the wisdom of the Japanese philosophy of the four life paths, we come to understand that fate and free will are not mutually exclusive. We learn to navigate the complexities of life by embracing both, recognising our agency in shaping our experiences and responses while accepting the larger cosmic forces at play.

WARRIOR ASSIGNMENT: As we navigate the paradox of fate and free will we begin to visualise higher frequencies. This practice involves cultivating a positive and empowering mindset through the use of visualisation techniques. Set aside a quiet moment each day to visualise yourself radiating with inner strength, resilience, and clarity of purpose. Imagine yourself transcending the limitations of external circumstances, aligning with your highest potential, and making choices that embody wisdom and virtue.

By consistently engaging in this practice, you raise your frequency, creating a ripple effect in your thoughts, emotions, and actions. Visualising higher frequencies enables you to transcend the limitations of the paradox, finding harmony and balance amidst the interplay of fate and free will.

Remember, the paradox is not a barrier but an invitation to explore the depths of our being, to unravel the mysteries of our existence, and to transcend the boundaries of our perceived limitations.

Embrace the paradox and discover the alchemical transformation that awaits you.

ENTRY 19

Paradox of progress & acceptance

"True progress lies not in the absence of challenges, but in the harmony between our pursuit of growth and our acceptance of what is. It is in the delicate balance between striving for improvement and finding contentment in the present moment that we discover the true path to fulfilment and inner peace." – Anonymous free thinker

Shouldn't we strive to improve ourselves? And how do we do that while accepting ourselves as we are? This paradoxical tension can be challenging but is ultimately rewarding.

The Stoics believed that failure was an essential part of personal growth and development, and that we should embrace it rather than fear it, but Certainly! Here's the continuation of the chapter on the paradox of progress and acceptance:

In the modern era, we find ourselves constantly striving for progress and improvement. We seek growth, success, and instant gratification in every aspect of our lives. However, within this pursuit of progress lies a paradox: the more we strive for advancement, the more we find ourselves longing for acceptance and contentment. As we explore the delicate balance between progress and acceptance, and how embracing the paradox can lead to a more fulfilling and meaningful life, have in mind how much you strive for a certain outcome, or how accepting you are of yourself and your journeys pace.

In today's fast-paced world, we have become accustomed to immediate results and instant gratification. We seek quick fixes, shortcuts, and rapid progress in all areas of our lives. However, this relentless pursuit of instant gratification often leads to frustration, dissatisfaction, and an inability to appreciate the present moment.

We must recognise the illusionary nature of instant gratification and embrace the concept of delayed gratification for true progress to unfold. I like everyone have been guilty of this chase and have battled to overcome the need for progress, but within the paradox inherently comes the paradox of letting you overcome the chase when you are ready to let go.

Our society's obsession with instant gratification has created an environment where impatience reigns supreme. We expect instant success, instant happiness, and instant fulfilment. We want to be enlightened after one meditation, we want a six pack after one workout, and we want our dream wife after one date. We want results without putting in the necessary time and effort. This mindset not only hinders our personal growth but also robs us of the joy and satisfaction that come from the journey itself. This is not to say that in some aspects of life things are granted to us instantly. In fact there could be a way to develop that, but this is something you can ask me in time. For now just enjoy the paradox and allow the knowledge to sink in.

Progress requires time, effort, and perseverance in many cases. It is through patience and persistence that we can navigate the challenging path of personal growth and development. Embracing the paradox of progress and acceptance means understanding that true progress often occurs gradually, and that setbacks and obstacles are inevitable along the way. By cultivating patience and embracing the journey, we can find a deeper sense of fulfilment and resilience.

In the face of adversity, it is our ability to persist and remain steadfast that allows us to overcome obstacles and continue on our path of progress. The Stoics believed in the power of perseverance and advocated for embracing challenges as opportunities for growth. By adopting a mindset of resilience and unwavering determination, we can navigate the ups and downs of life with grace and fortitude.

While progress is important, it is equally crucial to focus on the process rather than being fixated on the outcome. The Stoics believed in the importance of doing our best in any given situation, regardless of the ultimate result. By shifting our focus to the present moment and engaging fully in the process, we can find joy and fulfilment in the journey itself, regardless of the outcome.

When we become too fixated on the end result, we risk missing out on the valuable lessons and experiences that the process offers. It is through the process of growth that we learn, evolve, and develop as individuals. By embracing the journey and fully immersing ourselves in the present moment, we cultivate a sense of mindfulness and a deeper appreciation for the unfolding of life.

Acceptance does not mean complacency or resignation. It means acknowledging and embracing the reality of our current circumstances while maintaining the desire for growth and improvement. True acceptance allows us to let go of resistance and attachment to external outcomes, freeing us to focus on inner transformation and aligning our actions with our values and principles.

Acceptance is not about settling for less; it is about embracing what is while striving for what can be. It is about finding the serenity to accept the things we cannot change and the courage to change the things we can. By finding this balance between acceptance and ambition, we create a harmonious alignment between our desires and the realities of life.

The paradox of progress and acceptance lies in the understanding that true growth and fulfilment come from the delicate interplay between striving for progress and embracing acceptance. It is through this paradox that we can find harmony and a deeper sense of purpose in our journey.

By accepting the present moment and acknowledging our current circumstances, we create a solid foundation for growth. Acceptance allows us to see things as they are, without judgment or resistance. It is a powerful act of surrender, acknowledging that within the surrender comes an innate higher self-power that begins to thread seamlessly into daily life and our journeys progress.

Simultaneously, progress pushes us forward, encouraging us to stretch our limits, challenge ourselves, and reach for new heights. It is the driving force that fuels our ambition, propelling us toward personal and professional development. Progress allows us to tap into our potential and manifest our dreams into reality. This requires that we take action as part of the process and replacing habits and rituals that no longer serve us, to allow space in our life for accelerated growth.

However, it is crucial to recognise that progress does not equate to an endless pursuit of external achievements. True progress encompasses both inner transformation and external accomplishments. It involves developing our character, honing our skills, and cultivating virtues such as resilience, patience, and wisdom. It requires continuous self-reflection and the willingness to learn from both successes and failures.

To navigate the paradox of progress and acceptance, we must find a delicate balance between the two. We must embrace the process of growth, relishing the small victories along the way while remaining open to the lessons and insights that arise from acceptance. It is in this space of balance that we discover true fulfilment and a sense of wholeness.

It reminds us that life is a delicate dance between striving for growth and finding contentment in the present moment. It is through this dance that we can navigate the complexities of life, cultivate resilience, and find fulfilment on our journey.

As Stoic alchemists, we embrace the paradox and harness its transformative power. We understand that progress without acceptance leads to perpetual dissatisfaction, while acceptance without progress can lead to stagnation. By finding the delicate balance between the two, we can experience true growth, inner peace, and a sense of purpose.

May you embark on this journey of paradox with an open heart and a curious mind. Embrace the challenges, celebrate the victories, and trust in the wisdom that lies within you. Remember that the path of progress and acceptance is unique to each individual, and it is through your personal exploration that you will uncover the alchemical secrets to a fulfilled life.

Continue to embrace the paradox, and may your journey be filled with growth, acceptance, and the transformative power of progress.

WARRIOR ASSIGNMENT: To integrate the paradox of progress and acceptance into your life, I invite you to engage in a reflective practice. Take some time to contemplate the areas of your life where you feel the pull between progress and acceptance. Ask yourself:

1. What aspects of your life do you feel a strong desire to change or improve? These can be personal, professional, or relational areas.

2. Are there any areas where you struggle with acceptance, resisting the present moment or wishing things were different?

3. How can you find a balance between striving for progress and embracing acceptance in these areas? Consider the actions you can take and the mindset shifts you can cultivate.

Once you have gained clarity, choose one specific area to focus on. Create a plan that incorporates both progress-oriented actions and acceptance practices. Be kind and patient with yourself throughout the process.

I encourage you to journal about your experiences, noting any insights, challenges, or breakthroughs that arise. Remember, this is a journey of self-discovery and growth, and the paradox of progress and acceptance is a lifelong practice.

In modern times, embracing the paradoxes of life often involves accepting that life is full of ups and downs, successes and failures, joys and sorrows. It may involve recognising that our strengths can also be our weaknesses, and that our weaknesses can also be our strengths. It may involve acknowledging that we can experience

both happiness and sadness, and that these emotions are not
mutually exclusive.

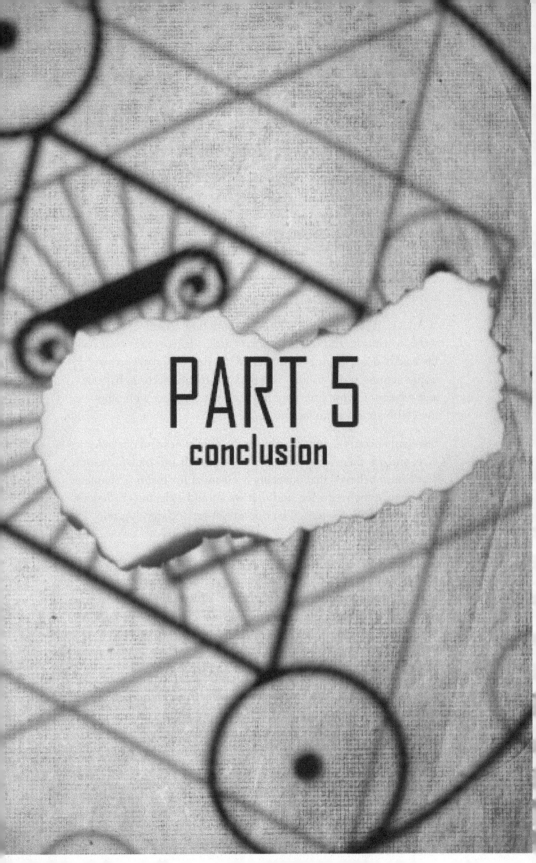

PART 5

conclusion

ENTRY 20

March forth Stoic Warrior

"It is not death that a man should fear, but he should fear never beginning to live." - Marcus Aurelius

We wind these final pages up with some stoic thoughts and transmutations we can make with daily life and what it can mean for us moving forward.

WARRIOR ASSIGNMENT: Take some time to reflect on and write down how you can incorporate Stoic alchemy into your daily life as a dad and a business owner. What practices can you start implementing today to help you find greater connection, balance, and wisdom in your life? And how can you connect with other men who are on a similar journey?

Stoicism encourages us to embrace the challenges and obstacles we face, and see them as opportunities for growth and transformation. The Stoics believed that adversity is essential for building character and developing resilience, and that we should welcome challenges as opportunities to strengthen our willpower and develop our virtues.

The creation of Stoic alchemy as a philosophy is a brainchild that combines the principles of Stoicism and alchemy to help us achieve greater happiness, success, and fulfilment in our lives. As men, we face many challenges and responsibilities, but by applying the principles of Stoic alchemy, we can find greater balance, connection, and purpose in our lives.

By exploring the concepts of connection, balance, and paradox, we can learn to connect more deeply with ourselves, our communities, and the natural world around us. We can find greater balance between activity and rest, logic and flow, and planning and creation. And we can learn to embrace the paradoxical elements of life, finding meaning and purpose in the challenges and contradictions that we face.

Through these practices we can transform our lives and continue on a journey that will keeps us content and in a constant state of open-hearted growth.

Stoic alchemy is a powerful framework for personal growth and development. By combining the ancient philosophy of Stoicism with the transformative practices of alchemy, we can cultivate deeper connections, find balance, and embrace life's paradoxes.

Throughout this book, we have explored the concepts of Stoic alchemy in depth, including Stoicism and alchemy themselves, the importance of connection and balance, and the paradoxical nature of life. By implementing the actionable tasks provided at the end of each chapter, you can begin to incorporate these concepts into your own life and experience the benefits for yourself.

By implementing the warrior assignments provided throughout this book, you can begin to incorporate these concepts into your own life and experience the benefits for yourself. Remember, personal growth and development is a lifelong journey, and by embracing the principles of Stoic alchemy, you can continue to grow and evolve as a man, a father, a business owner, and a human being.

Here I have offered a powerful framework for personal transformation and growth that can be especially helpful for your daily development. Whether you are struggling with stress, anxieties, depression, overwhelm, or simply seeking to deepen your sense of connection and purpose, Stoic Alchemy offers a path towards greater fulfilment and wellbeing. So, take some time to explore these principles for yourself, and see how they can help you unlock your own inner alchemist and transform your life from the inside out.

We hope that this book has been informative and inspiring, and that it will continue to help you on your journey towards greater happiness, success, and fulfilment. Remember to stay curious, stay open-minded, and stay true to yourself as you continue to explore Stoic alchemy and apply its principles to your own life.

ENTRY 21

Epilogue

So what happens next? We have embarked on a journey together, exploring the depths of Stoic Alchemy and its profound wisdom for personal transformation. We have delved into the paradoxes of life, uncovered the principles of connection, balance, and acceptance, and explored the path of the Stoic Warrior. Now, as we reach the conclusion of this book, it is time to reflect on what we have learned and consider how to apply these teachings in our lives going forward.

Stoic Alchemy is not merely an intellectual exercise or a philosophical theory to be pondered. It is a practical guide for living a more meaningful and fulfilling life. Throughout our exploration, we have encountered powerful concepts and practices that have the potential to ignite profound change within us. But as with any transformative journey, the true power lies in the application of these principles.

The Stoic Alchemist, the archetype we have embraced throughout this book, understands that true alchemy happens within. It is the transmutation of our own thoughts, emotions, and actions that allows us to rise above the challenges of life and find deeper meaning and purpose. It is the integration of Stoic philosophy and practical wisdom that empowers us to navigate the paradoxes of existence with grace and resilience.

In the Stoic Alchemist's path, there is no destination to reach, no final attainment of perfection. It is an ongoing process of growth, self-reflection, and refinement. It is about recognising that our journey is unique and ever-evolving, and that our true power lies in our ability to respond to the circumstances of life with wisdom, virtue, and resilience.

So, what happens next? It is up to you. The wisdom and insights shared in this book are tools for your own alchemical journey. They are invitations to explore, experiment, and integrate the teachings into your daily life. Each day presents an opportunity to practice the principles of Stoic Alchemy and to embody the Stoic Warrior within.

One crucial aspect of moving forward is to create a personal practice that supports your growth and development. It could be a morning routine of reflection and journaling, a regular meditation practice, or engaging in physical activities that align with the Stoic principles of discipline and resilience. Find what resonates with you and commit to it with dedication and consistency.

Another important aspect is cultivating a community of like-minded individuals who share your aspirations for personal growth and embody the Stoic virtues. Seek out Stoic circles, join online communities, or start your own discussion group. Surround yourself with individuals who inspire and support you on your journey. If you found this book insightful and feel that a stoic alchemy group is something you would like to look more into then go to www.stoicalchemist.com for more information on the stoic warriors groups and activities I provide to help the growth and development of men all over the world.

Furthermore, remember that Stoic Alchemy is not an isolated pursuit. It is intertwined with the interconnectedness of all things. As we navigate our individual paths, let us also extend our wisdom and compassion to others. Practice empathy, kindness, and understanding in your interactions with the world. Recognise the power you hold to uplift and inspire those around you.

As we conclude this book, it is essential to acknowledge that the journey of Stoic Alchemy is never truly complete. The paradoxes, challenges, and opportunities of life continue to unfold. Our understanding deepens, our wisdom expands, and our capacity for growth and transformation evolves.

So, my fellow Stoic Warriors, let us embrace the paradoxes, honour the journey, and commit ourselves to the ongoing pursuit of self-mastery and personal transformation. Let us continue to apply the principles of Stoic philosophy in our lives and strive to create a more compassionate, resilient, and virtuous world.

May our paths be guided by the principles of connection, balance, and acceptance. May we find solace in the paradoxes of life and draw strength from the Stoic Warrior within. And may the alchemical journey unfold with grace, purpose, and profound meaning.

As we conclude this book, I invite you to take a moment of reflection. Look back at how far you have come, acknowledge the progress you have made, and envision the path ahead. Embrace the paradoxes as opportunities for growth, and remember that the true alchemy happens within you.

Thank you for joining me on this transformative journey through my first book. May the wisdom of Stoic Alchemy continue to inspire and guide you on your path to self-discovery and personal fulfilment.

With unlimited gratitude,

Jase

And finally...

Here are a few more of the most profound stoic quotes that I love from various philosophers. And as a final WARRIORS ASSIGNMENT, I would encourage you to spend time pondering over their meanings and how each could impact your everyday life:

"The things you think about determine the quality of your mind. Your soul takes on the colour of your thoughts." - Marcus Aurelius

"We are not given a good life or a bad life. We are given a life. It is up to us to make it good or bad." – Unknown but often attributed to Marcus Aurelius

"The happiness of your life depends upon the quality of your thoughts." – Marcus Aurelius

"We must be willing to let go of the life we planned so as to have the life that is waiting for us." - Epictetus

"The art of living is more like wrestling than dancing." - Marcus Aurelius

"It is not that we have a short time to live, but that we waste a lot of it." - Seneca

"The obstacle is the way." - Ryan Holiday (inspired by the Stoic philosopher Epictetus)

"The wise man looks to the future, but enjoys the present." – Seneca

"Happiness is not something ready made. It comes from your own actions." - Dalai Lama XIV